Praise for **Changing the Way We Change**

"This is a great book packed with a balanced mixture of behavioral insights, practical wisdom, and change processes for winning. Anyone who is or should be pursuing change should have this book within easy reach."

H. Barry Bebb, PhD
Barry Bebb & Associates

"[*Changing the Way We Change*] is a comprehensive and very insightful treatment of change management. It is obvious that the author is a seasoned practitioner. The unique feature of this book is the dual focus on insight/understanding/wisdom with a practical tested approach."

Dr. Earl C. Young
Department of Management
DePaul University

"The material can be applied immediately. It is exciting. It generates new ideas and different ways of looking at change and its management."

Herman Zwirn
Director, Systems and Organizational Development
Helene Curtis, Inc.

Changing the Way We Change

*Gaining Control of
Major Operational Change*

Engineering Process Improvement Series

John W. Wesner, Ph.D., P.E., Consulting Editor

Lou Cohen
Quality Function Deployment:
How to Make QFD Work for You

William Y. Fowlkes/Clyde M. Creveling
Engineering Methods for Robust Product Design:
Using Taguchi Methods® in Technology and Product Development

Maureen S. Heaphy/Gregory F. Gruska
The Malcolm Baldrige National Quality Award:
A Yardstick for Quality Growth

Jeanenne LaMarsh
Changing the Way We Change:
Gaining Control of Major Operational Change

William J. Latzko/David M. Saunders
Four Days with Dr. Deming:
A Strategy for Modern Methods of Management

Rohit Ramaswamy
Design and Management of Service Processes

Richard C. Randall
Randall's Practical Guide to ISO 9000:
Implementation, Registration, and Beyond

John W. Wesner/Jeffrey M. Hiatt/David C. Trimble
Winning with Quality:
Applying Quality Principles in Product Development

Changing the Way We Change

Gaining Control of Major Operational Change

Jeanenne LaMarsh

ADDISON-WESLEY PUBLISHING COMPANY

Reading, Massachusetts   Menlo Park, California   New York
Don Mills, Ontario   Wokingham, England   Amsterdam   Bonn
Sydney   Singapore   Tokyo   Madrid   San Juan
Paris   Seoul   Milan   Mexico City   Taipei

Many of the designations used by manufacturers and sellers to distinguish their products are claimed as trademarks. Where those designations appear in this book and Addison-Wesley was aware of a trademark claim, the designations have been printed with initial capital letters.

The publisher offers discounts on this book when ordered in quantity for special sales.

For more information, please contact:
Corporate & Professional Publishing Group
Addison-Wesley Publishing Company
One Jacob Way
Reading, Massachusetts 01867

Library of Congress Cataloging-in-Publication Data

LaMarsh, Jeanenne, 1943–
   Changing the way we change : gaining control of major operational change /
Jeanenne LaMarsh.
      p.   cm. — (Engineering process improvement series)
   Includes bibliographical references and index.
   ISBN 0-201-63364-7 (acid-free paper)
   1. Organizational change—Management.   I. Title.   II. Series.
HD58.8.L36   1995
658.4′6—dc20   95-8317
                                                                                      CIP

0-201-63364-7

1 2 3 4 5 6 7 8 9-CRW-98979695
First printing May 1995

To All the KO's.

To NMO, with love and thanks.

Engineering Process Improvement Series

Consulting Editor, John Wesner, Ph.D., P.E.

Global competitiveness is of paramount concern to the engineering community worldwide. As customers demand ever-higher levels of quality in their products and services, engineers must keep pace by continually improving their processes. For decades, American business and industry have focused their quality efforts on their end products rather than on the processes used in the day-to-day operations that create these products and services. Experts across the country now agree that focusing on continuous improvements of the core business and engineering processes within an organization will lead to the most meaningful, long-term improvements and production of the highest-quality products.

Whether your title is researcher, designer, developer, manufacturer, quality or business manager, process engineer, student, or coach, you are responsible for finding innovative, practical ways to improve your processes and products in order to be successful and remain world-class competitive. The *Engineering Process Improvement Series* takes you beyond the ideas and theories, focusing in on the practical information you can apply to your job for both short-term and long-term results. These publications offer current tools and methods and useful how-to advice. This advice comes from the top names in the field; each book is both written and reviewed by the leaders themselves, and each book has earned the stamp of approval of the series consulting editor, John W. Wesner.

Key innovations by industry leaders in process improvement include work in benchmarking, concurrent engineering, robust design, customer-to-customer cycles, process management, and engineering design. Books in this series will discuss these vital issues in ways that help engineers of all levels of experience become more productive and increase quality significantly.

All of the books in the series share a unique graphic cover design. Viewing the graphic blocks descending, you see random pieces coming together to build a solid structure, signifying the ongoing effort to improve processes and produce quality products most satisfying to the customer. If you view the graphic blocks moving upward, you see them breaking through barriers—just as engineers and companies today must break through traditional, defining roles to operate more effectively with concurrent systems. Our mission for this series is to provide the tools, methods, and practical examples to help you hurdle the obstacles, so that you can perform simultaneous engineering and be successful at process and product improvement.

The series is divided into three categories:

Process Management and Improvement   This includes books that take larger views of the field, including major processes and the end-to-end process for new product development.

Improving Functional Processes   These are the specific functional processes that are combined to form the more inclusive processes covered in the first category.

Special Process Topics and Tools   These are methods and techniques that are used in support of improving the various processes covered in the first two categories.

Foreword

I've learned three things about managing change. Let me share them with you.

First, I've concluded that the pace of change is increasing, and is unlikely to slow in our lifetime. Many factors combine to ensure that we will all face significant change at a rate faster than ever before. Each business will face new and advancing technologies, growing customer demands, shifting competitor strategies, distribution and logistics capabilities advances, and a host of other factors . . . all at once. Beyond that, our global markets are profoundly affected by political shifts and global economic patterns, and have consequences for how we live and operate.

At Compaq, for example, we've seen change at a breakneck pace. A few short years ago, product developers in our industry thought in terms of years. Today, many Compaq products are conceived of, designed, manufactured, and supported in development cycles measured in a few months. The cycles are compressing further.

This intensification of change is by no means unique to the computer industry. We hear about the need for rapid adaptation from our customers around the world every day in the form of new requirements. No industry will be untouched; no part of the globe is immune.

Second, I've learned that organizations which develop a tolerance for change have a sustainable competitive advantage. At Compaq, we've invested heavily in the traditional assets that will help us succeed, such as technologies, development and manufacturing expertise, business processes, and a skilled workforce. We've made a sizable investment of another sort as well. We realize that a change-capable organization can be one of our greatest areas of advantage.

A workforce with an understanding of change can adapt to the needs of our marketplace. By building expertise in the management of change, we can flexibly and responsively meet future challenges.

While I don't know the specific products and services Compaq will offer five years from today, I can tell you that we will be ready to meet the challenges of the year 2000. We're banking on the fact that our people, combined with our other competitive strengths, will carry us forward in a consistently winning way.

Third, I've found that effective change rarely happens by chance. Just as it requires focus and concentration of effort to build an excellent manufacturing capability, for example, it requires focus and concentration of effort to embed a tolerance for change in a company's culture.

Changing the Way We Change can help your organization in a number of ways. Jeanenne LaMarsh will help you understand a systematic and logical way of thinking about change. You'll learn a lexicon of terms that will help you communicate with others about the issues involved with managing change. You'll gain an appreciation of the priority you need to place on having a clear future in mind and a solid footing from which to identify potential resistance. You'll learn by reviewing practical examples. You'll recognize the levers that must be pulled to manage change in your business situation.

For me the lessons are clear. Some will be defeated by the rapid pace of change. Some will face mediocrity because of their inability to respond. At Compaq, we intend to thrive on change. *Changing the Way We Change* will help you do the same.

Hans Gutsch
Senior Vice President,
 Human Resources
Compaq Computer Corporation

Preface

I have been a student of change for many years. I have watched companies, governments, and individual people struggle with change. Change can cause pain, and it can bring great joy. Because change is becoming an increasing force in our lives, I am convinced that the companies, governments, and individuals who understand and cope with change will take us into the future. If this book helps, use it.

My knowledge of change and the change process comes from a rich variety of thinkers cited in the following pages. This knowledge has been expanded, challenged, and enhanced by the people and companies I have worked with over the years. The lines between the teacher and student are often blurred. That is as it should be: understanding change is a constantly changing process.

This book is written to share with you what I know about change and how it can be managed. For many of you, incorporating this understanding will require a change in the way you have managed change; for others it will validate and help to organize what you have learned from your own experiences. For everyone, it will be an opportunity to determine how your companies are going to deal with change in the future.

The body of knowledge about change can be best understood by looking at it as four elements. Those elements form the structure and organization of this book:

- The process of change
- The people in that process
- The systems that support change
- The planning to make change happen

To help you understand and relate to those key elements, I have looked at each from three different perspectives. Every chapter in the book is divided into three sections—a discussion of the key change element, which is entitled Element of Change; a story about a company experiencing a major change and how it copes with each of these elements, entitled Real World Example; and a set of tools to help you deal with that element in your own origination, entitled Tools for Change.

Putting this learning into a book was a task made easier by several people. I cannot thank them enough for their insights, criticisms, and support. Heath Izenson came to me fresh out of the University of Michigan and changed me. He helped me to tighten up my writing style and, most important, he challenged my thinking about the whole change process. He continues to do that and often moves faster than I do to absorb and integrate new thinking about change. Heath has reminded me what change is like and I thank him for that.

My partner, John Karnatz, made great changes for himself and for LaMarsh & Associates as this manuscript was being prepared. Those changes also had a profound impact on my thinking about change and how to share my observations and knowledge with the reader. John, too, will continue to influence and challenge my thinking about change and I thank him also.

I also thank the following reviewers: Barry Bebb, William Bridges, Sandra Harrison, Gary Kissler, Craig Lundberg, Mark Michaels, Charles Savage, Michael Sheahan, Debbie Steffenson, John Wesner, Earl Young, and Herman Zwirn.

I am very grateful to Jennifer Joss of Addison-Wesley for her support and advice in the development of this book. Jennifer made sure that we worked as partners and always made me feel as though I had a great support system behind me as I struggled to find a way to help people understand how to make change happen.

Contents

1
Introduction

CHANGE AND CHANGE MANAGEMENT

Change was once a discrete event with a beginning, middle, and end. At the end things got back to "normal." Today, change is a constant; multiple changes happen simultaneously with no "normal" in sight. Changes can take companies and the people in them toward a successful future, into a limbo of change for changes' sake, or into oblivion. What makes the difference? The successful organization is agile and responsive, taking advantage of changes in market, technologies, and processes. Knowing what change to make, building a high tolerance for change, and understanding how to make change happen will give your company a major competitive advantage.

Change is not the enemy. It can unlock the possibilities for future success. This book is about the effective continuous change management capabilities that help companies and people change easily and well, thus enabling the organization to profit from new opportunities. As a student of change for almost two decades, I have watched change move from an isolated event to a constant for my clients. Without a comprehensive change management strategy there is little hope for a future.

Like so many important business concepts, change management has become trivialized and diluted by being given a multitude of meanings. Change management loses its impact and usefulness without the proper tools to understand and practice it.

Change management is the methodology that hardwires change and the ability to adapt into the organization. It includes applying change-related research and experience in a systematic way to every business project. It means building systematic thought about change into every business decision. It requires organizing this knowledge about change into a repeatable, teachable framework that is constantly refined and improved. Changes become an integral part of the way companies work and the springboard for more and constant change.

Change management is *not* training. It is *not* communication. It is *not* process analysis and re-design. Change management is a key competency that must be built into the very fabric of the company; a structured methodology that *incorporates* training, communicating, listening, and process analysis and re-design. It is a way of thinking that becomes part of defining the organization.

INSTINCTIVE VERSUS LEARNED CHANGE MANAGEMENT

Many companies and individuals are good at change. Scattered throughout companies are change agents, people who seem to know just what to do to make change happen right. It is as if they have an antenna that alerts them to all the right questions, issues, and concerns. Those who are not as good at causing or coping with change look at them with wonder. How did they know to watch for signs that the customer would have a problem with the new order processing system? Why did that speech announcing the change generate so much enthusiasm in the whole organization?

Some companies (perhaps your competitors are among them) manage to introduce major changes in technology, reduce head count by 35 percent, and drastically reduce time to market without causing wrenching reactions from the workers. Their changes have dramatically high success rates, with fast results and relatively low costs in dollars, disruption, and pain.

What are those companies doing and why? To make change happen effectively in your company, you need to understand what those change agents and companies seem to know instinctively. Change management can be learned by understanding and optimizing the processes and people involved. A process is a path of action that can be described, diagrammed, understood, and replicated. People and their relationships to change can also be described, diagrammed, understood, and replicated.

A PREDICTION

Change has become a constant, and it is not going away. The status quo will be the status quo for about 20 minutes. Constant, wrenching, good, or bad; people have to learn to live with all kinds of changes. The question is not whether to change; standing still means being left behind. But success hinges on choosing the right changes and implementing them quickly and well. Companies and individuals who can implement change successfully will succeed in the marketplace.

Flexibility is fast becoming a major competitive weapon. The company that cannot change will not survive. Therefore *change cannot be left to chance!*

A PRESCRIPTION

If your company is serious about success you must:

1. Commit to making change a key element in the culture of the company.
2. Understand that change drivers are in the market and cannot be ignored.
3. Build a systematic change management methodology.
4. Integrate that methodology into the heart of the organization.

This methodology must become the way you *do* change. It means holding change agents accountable for developing and enhancing this methodology and applying it repeatedly. People who develop these skills and knowledge must become the most important people in your company.

WHY USE CHANGE MANAGEMENT?

Companies have learned over the past few years that they must make major changes in their organization, focus, use of people, and design and delivery of products and services. These years have brought some incredibly powerful tools for remaking companies through overarching, broad changes that affect the whole organization and accelerate successful achievements. Unfortunately, problems related to poor change management have dampened these tools' success.

Quality circles were the hottest management trend in the 1980s. But in spite of their potential, they seemed to fade away. In June of 1993, 400 plant safety engineers assembled in a room in Dallas to talk about change and change management. Before the session began, I surveyed those 400 people. How many of them worked for companies that introduced quality circles? Four hundred hands went up.

Second question: how many of those companies were successful in implementing quality circles? Not a single hand went up!

Third question: how many were working for companies that were currently trying to implement Total Quality Management, Empowered Employees, Reengineering, or a combination of those initiatives? Again, as with quality circles, every hand in the room went up.

Then, the fourth question: how many expected to return to this room in two years and report major success in their new projects? Four hundred people in the room. *Five* hands went up!

The scars of failed change endeavors are far reaching. A few months ago, I was walking down the corridor of the corporate offices of a bank in New York City. Waiting for me in the conference room was the Customer Service Task Force, assigned the responsibility of changing the organization's thinking about customer service. The task force leader hurrying down the hall beside me casually remarked, "Oh, by the way, be sure when you get in there not to mention anything about Total Quality Management. We tried that last year and it was a dismal failure. We have been forbidden by our president to use that phrase. He wants us to forget that failure and concentrate on this new change."

Quality circles, TQM, and business process reengineering are major changes that affect everyone in the company. Those 400 people in Dallas and the task force leader at the bank are really saying that global changes require a structured method to gain control over and manage change.

Some powerful change tools are now available to companies who are serious about success. Business process reengineering is being applied from Fortune 100 companies to government departments to small service businesses. This tool effectively challenges every aspect of the way work is done and determines a better way to make the process flow. Many dollars are spent in reengineering. Many organizations, however, do not realize the increased productivity, profitability, and customer satisfaction they hoped to see as a payback on their investment.

Overarching Changes

Processes cannot be looked at in isolation. Fundamental overarching changes in any organization require change agents to understand and integrate changes required in *process, structure, people,* and *culture* within a vision. Margaret Wheatley, in *Leadership and the New Science,* calls that vision an invisible force of unseen connections among those four components.

In their book *Reengineering the Corporation,* Michael Hammer and James Champy identify the changes that result from rethinking processes:

- Jobs expand.
- People make more of their own choices and decisions.
- People work more in teams.
- Managers become coaches.
- Whole departments disappear.
- Workers focus on the customer, not on the manager.
- Workers focus on the process, not on the function.

These changes are not accomplished by presenting a flowchart or making an announcement. They deeply affect people. If you don't deal with that human factor and make revisions within the framework of a vision they will not succeed. Reengineering is already being criticized as another "quick fix dreamed up by consultants," and a method to get rid of people. If companies don't successfully implement the changes identified by reengineering, this valuable tool will go the way of quality circles.

All changes, the overarching and the specific, must be identified and integrated to manage change effectively. Overarching changes have an impact at the macro level, affecting the company, its customers, competitors, and environment. At the same time, the impact cascades down until it affects every individual (Figure 1.1). To succeed with new efforts, companies have to build a high tolerance for the fact that implementation causes flexible and fluid changes. Then they can design an effective strategy to implement the operational, organizational, and people changes at each level.

Specific Changes

Every global company change is composed of individual, specific changes that must be implemented. The new order-processing system, the shop-floor reorganization, the meeting between distribution and main office management to discuss more effective product shipment and new customer input avenues—each of these is a specific change from past operations, and each must be managed.

Poorly managed, these changes fail. The new order-processing system begins to look remarkably like the old one. The work-flow reorganization costs thousands of dollars just for moving equipment, not counting line downtime and the re-design team's salary. Yet six months later there is no increase in productivity, and workers spend time bickering, fighting, and demanding that management make their lives easier.

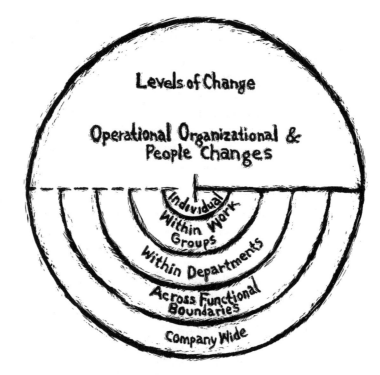

Figure 1.1
Cascading Impact of Change

THE DECISION TO MANAGE CHANGE

Managing change is expensive. At least it looks like that at the front end. It takes time to develop a methodology and put it in place. It takes time to use it—to plan the change and pay attention to the change elements addressed in the methodology. Time costs money.

Managing change takes energy. The systematic application of a change management methodology is not an easy process. It will take a considerable amount of energy to put it in place.

Do not order up a change management strategy unless you really need it. If you can make change happen to your level of satisfaction without all this additional energy and cost, by all means do so—but make that decision after careful analysis.

A COMPETITIVE EDGE

It is hoped that you are doing enough competitive analysis to know where you are in relation to your competition:

- Are you better or worse than your competition at satisfying the customer?
- Are you holding your own in market share?
- Are you increasing?
- Decreasing?
- How fast are you getting new products to markets compared to them?
- How long is your lead time on current product delivery relative to theirs?

You want to stay ahead of the competition, but there is no guarantee that your company can implement the good ideas that would give you the leading edge. So there is one more question to ask about your competitors:

- How good are they at managing the changes that will deliver *them* the competitive edge?

Even if you already manage changes well, it is critical to unify and integrate the knowledge, resources, and tools of change management scattered throughout the company into a comprehensive structured methodology. Without that structured methodology, there is a good possibility that even the best change agents will skip steps in the process. They certainly cannot guarantee repeating the process consistently if they have not identified all the steps. Equally important, change agents need to replicate themselves, to build a critical mass of change agents within the company. Charles Savage in *Fifth Generation Management* says the organization itself must become a "changing agent," responding to and dialoging with its markets. There must be a process to teach everyone in the organization about change.

The latest change tools are common knowledge, accessible to your competitors as easily as they are to you. They know, as you do, about improving engineering processes, involving employees, doing major whiteboard thinking about streamlining processes and upgrading the systems. They understand, as you do, that they have to give customers what they want. They know they must develop an integrated product design and development methodology, and they see how concurrent engineering and quality function deployment are tools to make that happen.

What gives any one company a competitive edge when everyone knows what they should look like? Change management is that competitive edge. Recent

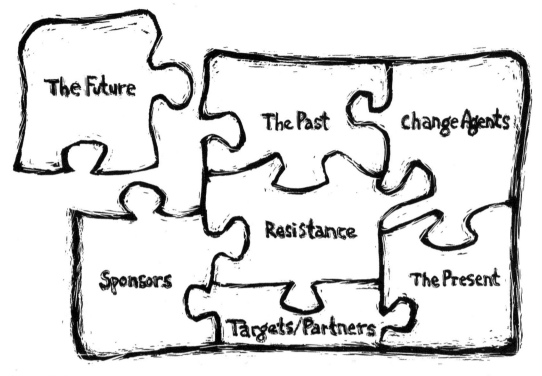

Figure 1.2
The Change Puzzle

history, the safety engineers in Dallas, and the changes you have tried to implement in your own company tell us that just knowing what to do is *not* enough. You must *make* change happen.

Building a systematic change management strategy into your plans will increase your payback from change efforts. It will ensure that the specific changes going on are integrated into your overarching change efforts. It will show the company, your customers, and your competitors that you know how to make change happen. Change management will give you the competitive edge.

THE CHANGE PUZZLE

Change is a challenge. Managing change is a skill. Skilled workers use the right tools, and change agents are no exception. Effective change agents use knowledge and application processes as their tools.

Knowledge of change and the change process can be identified in discrete elements (Figure 1.2). Of course, as in any complex human interaction, these elements blend and overlap and are never completely clean and predictable, but looking at them as individual parts of a whole will improve your understanding. Understanding the elements and their relationship to the whole leads to managed change.

HOW TO USE THIS BOOK

To successfully build change management into your company you need to understand what it is and determine how to use it. This book breaks change management down into four critical elements, which are listed as the four major parts of the book.

These four parts are as follows:

Part 1

The Change Process discusses the three time frames of the change process:

- The Future
- The Present
- The Delta

In this part you will examine what motivates changes and how to adjust the balance of change.

Part 2

The People Part of the Change Process defines the specific jobs that individuals and groups have in the change process:

- Sponsors
- Change Agents
- Targets

It also defines the ideal function of each of these roles and how to build those functions into your organization.

Part 3

The Tools of Change: The Change Systems lays out the fundamental elements of the three major change systems:

- Communication System
- Learning System
- Reward and Reinforcement System

Part 4

Putting It All Together: The Implementation Plan integrates these major change variables into an integrated implementation plan that defines roles and responsibilities, timelines, and action plans.

THREE APPROACHES TO UNDERSTANDING CHANGE MANAGEMENT

Each change element presented in the chapters is addressed in three ways:

1. Discussion of the critical change element
   - No one becomes a change agent without some understanding and experience with the change process. However, whether you are an extraordinarily successful change agent or are recently appointed and wondering what you have gotten yourself into, an in-depth look at each change element will help you gain a better understanding of each aspect and how they fit together.
2. The change elements in the real world
   - Treetop Manufacturing Company, like your organization and thousands of others, is trying to stay successful. Like you, it is trying to make large, overarching changes in the way it does business. It is also making minor and major specific changes in departments, processes, tools, and systems.
   - You can examine the efforts of Treetop and their change agents, Charlie and Sarah. By looking at what they do right and wrong, you can use Treetop as a template for reviewing what you are doing right and wrong in your own organization.
3. Tools of change
   - A methodology of any kind requires tools for implementation. This section will give you a toolbox of assessment instruments, checklists, and planning formats to use in building change management structure into your changes.

ACCOUNTABILITY AND THE FUTURE

If your company is going to survive and succeed, the ability to implement change successfully must become a critical part of your job description, no matter what your job function. Smart companies are building that requirement into their job descriptions; they are hiring people with proven change agent track records. They are building change agent accountability into their performance review systems, and they are training people to be change agents. They know they need effective change agents.

Effective change agents know how to manage change. This book helps build change agents who can create agile organizations that will lead the future.

PART ONE

The Change Process: A Journey Without End

Change does not just happen; it is driven. There are reasons that organizations and people change. The first step of change management is understanding the forces of change and learning to use those forces to your advantage.

Change is movement *away* from the present. It is movement *through* a place that is neither old nor new, the delta. The way things were was never firm; it was in a constant state of tension between the need to remain stable and the need to respond to time and its inevitable changes.

Inventory was once an asset, but over time inventory maintenance costs increased and product life cycles shortened. Companies realized that receivables were better than inventory. Finally, someone said, "Let's change. Let's start figuring out how to reduce inventory and get the product made and shipped to the customer at just the right time." A change began. The stability of years of thinking spilled into the chaos of the delta.

The delta, the transition from the way it was to the way it is going to be, is not a safe, well-defined path. Confusion, uncertainty, and lack of definition describe the delta. Those characteristics are the price paid for change. They are also the assets of the delta. People need the ability to move freely within the wide boundaries of the delta. This flexibility allows individuals and organizations to experiment, to test new future designs, and to find faster, easier ways to achieve future goals. Inventory reduction efforts have followed many paths that have led to other changes, from new ways of thinking about WIP (Work in Process) to new locations for truck-loading bays.

The future is not a firm, fixed place in time and definition. Simply going through the delta will alter and redefine the future. Factors that surface

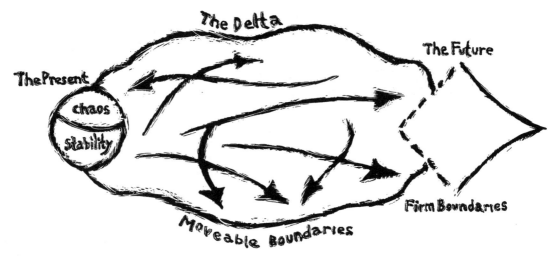

Figure P1.1
From the Present to the Future

throughout the delta affect your company's definition of the future. You can't ensure implementation that definitely follows a rigid set of changes. But the definition *does* have a shape. It has boundaries to keep your change efforts within the scope of your vision/mission (Figure P1.1).

Boundaries limit the types of changes chosen by the organization, and are subject to constant evaluation and adaptation. The company's vision/mission and operating principles define their boundaries. However, the company's organization, product mix, and physical location are elements that smart companies allow to remain loose and free, subject to challenge and constant change.

The change process is movement. It has boundaries, but it is also flexible and fluid.

The future, present, and delta have unique characteristics that the change agent needs to understand and use to ensure successful change.

2
Starting at the End—The Future

THE PARADOX

The future is a paradox. No one ever gets there: it is an elusive target that keeps slipping out of reach. If you could define your company's future clearly, the change process would be easier, but a detailed definition closes off unanticipated opportunities. Spending too much time on definitions may cut you off from the opportunities you do know about. Customer demands and competitive challenges may drive your initial change goals. But, as you work, you may discover ways to go *beyond* customer demands, anticipating and delighting customers. You can never know enough at the front end of a change to define it thoroughly, and you can't wait until you know enough. You can't reach a point and say, "We have achieved. We are done changing!"

You can use what you know about the future to launch change in the right direction. The future has a shape or boundaries, even if those boundaries shift and change. Motorola's boundaries changed: it used to be a company that made television sets. Hamilton Manufacturing in Two Rivers, Wisconsin, changed its line from wooden linotype to medical cabinets. The very act of changing alters and adjusts your future. The future is never an "end"—instead it is a guideline, a flexible framework that sets the outside boundaries for changes. It is ill defined, adjusting, and impermanent (see Figure 2.1).

People do try to fix an end to the future. Each change starts with an ending. People look at what they are losing and try to compare it to the future by asking endless questions: Where are we going? What will it look like? How will it be

15

Figure 2.1
The Impermanent, Adjusting Future

measured? Who will be there? What will the work flow look like there? What tools will we use? What data will our systems give us? What will we take with us from the present?

When people look from where they are to where they are being asked to go, they ask: Do I want to go there? To a large degree, the answer depends on what they see. It is a big decision. If the future is unclear, heading that way is risky. People want to know where they are going. When the future cannot be defined, people will endure incredible pain to stay in the present simply because they know and understand it. Fail to set the outside boundaries of the future and people trying to change may never leave or may end up in places you never intended.

How does a company deal with this dilemma? A detailed definition of the future limits opportunity and closes off future change. On the other hand, people find it easier to stay in the present than to head toward a loosely defined future. Insights from quantum physics and the theories of complexity and chaos can help you understand more about this paradox.

Organisms, from one-celled amoebas to multinational corporations, have a strong need for organization. They will form into a structure, but those structures must be fluid and flexible or the organism will die. The most effective structures seem to be those that can constantly adapt and revise themselves through incoming data. The virtual corporation, agile manufacturer, and company in perpetual redesign are always in transition, but changes driven by feedback stay within boundaries. How are those boundaries set? In the most effective organizations they are set by the framework of the future. Call it a vision, a mission, or guiding principles; it sets up the outside parameters within which the organization constantly changes, struggling between stability and chaos.

The current boundaries give you a picture of an organization's future:

- Number 1 in 1996
- World-Class Manufacturer
- The Supplier of Choice in Our Industry
- Quality is Our Job

Some logical elements are an inherent part of the future: a focus on quality, customers, change management, and empowered employees. Products, markets, structure, and processes may go through many unpredictable changes, but some core elements will probably remain stable and serve as boundaries far into the future.

> **A**fter the fall of the Soviet Union, America waited for *Cuba* to give up its Communist régime, but several years after the Berlin Wall came down, Fidel Castro was still firmly entrenched in Cuba. While there were some capitalistic initiatives, the people of Cuba seemed little inclined to make major changes, even though their economy was in chaos and many people were starving. The major problem seemed to be that the people of Cuba and their leaders could not *see* the future. They could not picture a future where their needs were met by a democratic, free-market economy. According to Johanna McGeary, writing in *Time* magazine about her tour of Cuba in the fall of 1993, the people of Cuba "want reform, but they don't know what kind. . . . The results are schizophrenic. The government promotes Cubacel, a joint telephone venture with Mexican businessmen—and the government organizes a new category of medals called Combatants of the Revolution to keep old-think alive."

> *Russia* itself is coping with the same basic problem. Boris Yeltsen decided to move Russia very aggressively toward the future. One of his major mistakes, however, was not helping the Russian people set parameters for that future and learn tolerance of the unknown. The Russian people have a fuzzy understanding of the free market and democracy, but Yeltsen has done little to help them to picture it at the national level and in their own homes. The Russian people cannot see that the future is a moving target, and that it has some inherent elements that are different from their past. It is hard for them to trust that Yeltsen can be the change agent to get them there.

A DEEPER DEFINITION

No one can be forced to change. Every individual in the company will make a choice. They will either:

- Choose to change
- Choose to stay with the old way
- Choose to try blocking or modifying the change

How do the people asked to change pick an option? They start by deciding if they can visualize the future that the company presents to them. Then they decide if they want to go there. They need to believe that the company is serious about the future and see that the future is a framework of boundaries that limit the changes that will be made. If they can do these things, they will be much more inclined to choose to change.

The Overarching Change

Much has been written about the importance of strategic planning, of setting a vision and mission to give the organization focus and a framework for the future. That vision/mission must define the business of the organization and identify key results and performance measurements that will determine the future's boundaries.

A vision can be depicted as an umbrella (Figure 2.2). It defines the broad framework of the future company. That umbrella is made up of individual spokes and connecting fabric: the elements that define *process, structure, people,* and *culture* in the future. When people look at the umbrella, from the inside or outside, they recognize it. Everyone can see the overarching picture of the future

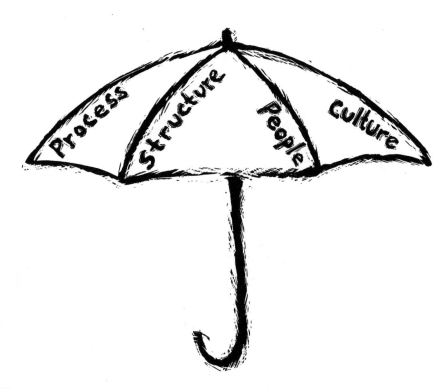

Figure 2.2
The Overarching Vision

organization and the degree and type of changes needed to achieve it. Over time, the umbrella may change its size, its color, its spoke alignment, or even its fabric type, but people operating inside and outside the company can still recognize the umbrella as unique to the company.

Most companies at least put the future into a picture of some kind and hang it on the wall. Yet these same companies often do not achieve successful change. Every office, the cafeteria, even the rest rooms have beautifully framed pictures of a graphic depicting the vision/mission. Gears, pyramids, mobius curves, inverted pyramids, and elaborate diagrams show the pictorial representation of the future. Employees carry laminated cards with the same representation in their wallets or pockets. The picture of the future is embossed on stationary, the annual report, mugs, and pens; it is even integrated into the company logo.

The frames on the walls start to get dusty. They slip a little and hang crooked. Nobody straightens them because nobody notices: everybody has stopped looking at the future. In some organizations, the frames even fall off the wall and drop behind a credenza or a bookcase. Nobody pays attention because everybody lost faith in the future a long time ago. They forgot there even was a future on the wall.

Yet changes are occurring—but many changes never really "take." Many changes head in directions that months later don't make sense, so they are aborted.

Change at a Functional Level

Change in the Engineering Department

The vice president of operations calls the entire engineering department together to announce a major change. He presents a new way of looking at design, manufacturability, and the working relationship of engineering, R&D, and suppliers. The engineers in the room recognize they are on their way to the future, but they have many questions. How do these changes fit into a future that makes sense to them? Are the required changes logical? How long will it take to get there? What kind of resources will they have to travel from here to there? How firm is "there?" Each engineer in the room looks at the change from his or her own perspective. "Will there be a place for me when we get there? If there is, will it be a place I will like?"

The changes required in engineering will be based on those four interrelated department aspects: *process, structure, people,* and *culture.* A change in any one aspect sets off changes in every other one. Therefore framing the change and fitting it into a larger future must start by looking at engineering as an entity made up of *process, structure, people,* and *culture.* Then each proposed change in any one aspect must be examined to determine its impact on the other three.

For example, the department might consider introducing a more sophisticated CAD system that affects *process.* The tool can dramatically reduce cycle time, but the current engineering department may not be structured to support the new system by taking more responsibility for the total design process. The department's structure will also need flexibility, so that management sign-offs can be adjusted for each type of design.

In what ways will the changes being considered alter the department's *structure,* the way management, engineers, and support personnel interact? Will it result in changes in reporting relationships? What physical and operational structures will be affected?

What about the *people*? Will the older engineers adjust? Will they have difficulty learning to use the system? Will the difference in acceptance by the older and younger engineers cause dissension among them? What will the learning curve be? Will people sit in different configurations? Will they have to give up the organization they have developed around their work station? How will they use their time differently?

Does the current *culture* support the introduction of a major new way of designing parts? What are the things people value most about the department and how it gets its work done? Who are the real heroes around the department—the innovative people who are always trying new things, or the two or three engineers who seem to know exactly where that old blueprint is and how to modify the new ones so the part can be machined just like the old?

Company-Wide Change

Even when the changes in engineering are well defined, the vice president of operations has another problem. The changes in engineering had better fit into the company's picture of where it is going. If this department's changes do not integrate with all the other changes going on in the company, the vice president might implement a major change that does not fit into the framework of the future. The resulting confusion and mixed signals about the company's destination scatter change efforts, eat up resources, and prevent the organization from moving in the right direction.

At that macro level, the company as a whole, the four areas of concern continue to be *process, structure, people,* and *culture.* When the lead time for design is shortened, what will the impact on scheduling people be? Engineers suddenly empowered to make more autonomous decisions not only find their relationship with their own management affected; they also run smack into the management structure out on the shop floor, which is not used to working with the engineer directly.

Will the rest of the company's structure be ready to optimize the shortened cycle time for drawings? Will it be able to take advantage of the engineer's new ability to do "what if's" in seconds instead of hours? How did the culture of the company perceive engineering in the past? Will it be able to absorb a shift in the relationship between engineering and the rest of the company?

MAKING A COMMITMENT

Developing a vision/mission statement and the picture representing it is important. Putting that picture on the wall and on everyone's coffee mug is a good change management technique. Expecting the needed changes to happen as a result of these activities is stupid. Good change agents know there is a body of activities that must kick in when the picture goes up on the wall and the decision is made that *this* is where the company is going. Senior management must understand that they cannot simply order change.

Change management starts with a strong management commitment to the future and a high tolerance for ambiguity in the delta of change. Tolerance means understanding that the future is a moving target to be watched and challenged. It also means understanding that changes are a necessary part of success. Near changes can be defined, resourced, and managed. Changes in the far future need to be welcomed and challenged. Senior management must do what it takes to make the adjustments that will achieve the vision/mission. That commitment must translate into specific activities to ensure these changes happen. One of those key activities is to apply organized, structured methodology to the change process.

REFINING THE DEFINITIONS

Tying down the future is not really possible. Even setting the framework is hard. Companies run into a problem regarding the future because the vision/mission statement is made up of words. The words are interpreted differently by each individual who sees or hears them. The senior management who sign off on those words frequently do not check with each other to see if they have the same understanding of what the words mean. Everyone involved needs to define each term in the vision/mission statement very carefully. They then need to share their interpretations and gain consensus for a common vision/mission.

- *Empowered employees*—how empowered? Does this mean the customer service advisor is empowered to promise immediate delivery to the customer yelling in his ear and can go right to the line to adjust the schedule? Does it mean eliminating the customer service advisor and letting the customer call to the shop floor supervisor directly? Will there even *be* a shop floor supervisor?
- *Customer satisfaction*—how much satisfaction? Does this mean the customer actually flies to our corporate offices and sits in on our product design meetings? Or does it just mean taking a more active role in soliciting their concerns and frustrations before starting the design phase? Charles Savage in *Fifth Generation Management* talks about customer significance. Tom Peters in *Thriving on Chaos* talks about customer delight. Does the company need to go that far? Is that the future? Does everyone know what those words mean? Do they mean the same thing to everyone?

- *Teamwork*—how much teamwork? Does this mean that people work more cooperatively within their work groups or does it mean knocking down the walls between departments and completely reorganizing the operation?

If the spokes and connecting fabric of the umbrella are not carefully spaced there will be little change. Senior management needs to determine up front whether there are parameters in which the vision/mission is to operate. Each level in the management cascade will deliver the vision/mission. If there are slight differences at the beginning between the finance vice president and the director of engineering, those differences might be vast by the time they get from North Carolina to Kansas or from the corporate office to the loading dock.

INTEGRATING THE CHANGES

Name all the changes going on in your organization today. The list is probably very long. A new operating system is being installed. There is an effort to create self-managed work teams. The marketing department is being reengineered. The engineering department is building a cross-functional team with R&D and learning to use Quality Function Deployment. The company has just cemented a joint venture with a South Korean firm, and there is some talk about buying out a small competitor with some exciting new technologies for manufacturing.

Each of these changes was determined to be good for the company. Think about the changes in your company. Look at your picture of the vision/mission. Does each of these changes help achieve that vision/mission? Is its contribution clear? Is it clear to everyone in the company? Can everyone look at all the ongoing changes and see how each contributes to the future? Can they see how each change relates to every other change, and how separate pieces fit together into a comprehensive whole?

Managing change does not mean a narrow, lock-step approach that controls all the change variables. Managing change means setting boundaries around the chaos, challenging the changes, and providing a process for continuing examination and redefinition within the framework of the vision/mission. Making sure each change fits into the framework of the future is critical, as is the need to constantly assess all changes against each other. Do these changes have a natural sequence? Do they have a logical sequence? Do they overlap? Draw upon common resources? A simple way to answer these questions is to create a fishbone diagram. (Figure 2.3) The future is the head of the fish. The spines are the current changes.

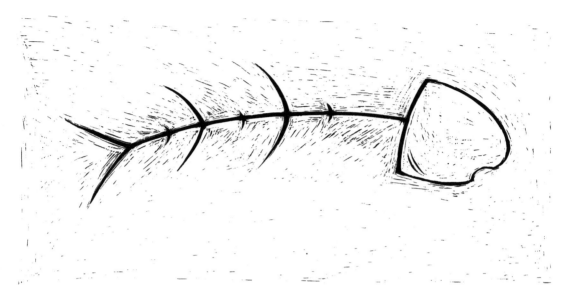

Figure 2.3
Defining All of the Changes

Using a fishbone diagram as an exercise can serve as an excellent reality check of whether the right changes are being made. It also helps senior management and everyone else see how these changes contribute to the future. The diagram serves as a catalyst for better planning and resource allocation.

A few years ago, *Millipore Corporation,* a Fortune 500 company outside of Boston, decided to make a major change: a full data swap from an IBM-based environment to a UNIX environment operating with Oracle software. It was a major change for this manufacturer of air and liquid filters. The decision had very strong sponsorship from the chief financial officer, who set tight time frames and an aggressive implementation schedule.

The task force assembled for implementation understood what they were charged to do, but one of the first questions this primary change agent group asked itself was, "What are we *really* doing? What change are we making here?" The team understood that software and hardware are tools. What would happen to Millipore when these tools were installed? They looked at the new tools and saw that the major change was a relational database that gave a lot of different people access to common information. They saw, as a result of this tool, that the company had an opportunity to adapt and modify the way it was organized, the way it used information internally and with customers, and the way it communicated across its global network. Millipore could build an integrated set of common business practices throughout the world. Is this what Millipore wanted? Did this fit with its vision/mission? Is this what senior management saw as the real change? Yes.

Now the Millipore Implementation Team had its change. It was a major change that contributed to achieving Millipore's vision/mission. The team could see its place in the larger picture. The changes they were implementing did not just mean information available in different ways to different people. Ultimately, it would mean shifts in the structure of the company: in the work processes, timing, number of employees, and employee skill sets. It would also mean changes in the Millipore culture: how people acted, what they considered important, what rules they followed, and what they believed. All those changes were not fully identified at the time the team began its work, but knowing those were the ultimate changes resulting from a new information system enabled the team to be more effective change agents.

Harris Trust and Savings Bank in Chicago has a vision/mission. It is expressed in a set of gears that mesh together to move Harris always closer to satisfying their customers. The individual gears are:

- Developing and empowering people
- Delivering value through teamwork
- Managing processes
- Continuously improving
- Eliminating waste

Harris also has a strong commitment to managing diversity. It is determined to encourage diversity in its workforce and to manage that diversity well. That commitment requires constant change throughout the organization as people learn more about diversity and how to manage it. The company has implemented education and training regarding ethnic, religious, and gender differences. It has changed its performance appraisal system to hold people accountable for managing diversity well.

That effort is succeeding. A key reason is that Harris understands that managing diversity makes good business sense. It is the right thing to do, *and* it contributes to the vision/mission hanging on the wall in every office and conference room in the company.

Managing diversity contributes to the development and empowerment of people. It contributes to the ability of people to deliver value through teamwork. It makes managing processes easier and more effective when people can deal with their differences. It means the organization has a better chance to constantly improve and eliminate waste because one of the greatest wastes of all has been eliminated—the waste that comes when people cannot work together because they are different.

BENCHMARKING AND HOLODECKS AND WHAT-IF'S . . .

There are a variety of excellent techniques available to address the difficulty of defining the future. Exercises to define the vision/mission can be found in countless good books. Benchmarking is excellent for identifying future possibilities and initiating discussion and consensus building about the organization's future. Looking at other organizations, walking around in them, talking to people, and examining their processes and tools helps build a picture of the future. Benchmarking also provides some solid, measurable elements of the future. This is critical to a successful change.

A word of caution about benchmarking: When going to other companies to study what they have achieved, be sure to pay particular attention to whether the organizational, operational, and procedural changes have also resulted in *real* changes. Are people working within the new paradigm or struggling to get the old one back? What effect does achieving the future have on people: more or less job satisfaction, more or less control?

Are you a Trekkie? Fans of *Star Trek: The Next Generation* know the crew has a very special way to entertain themselves. They do not sit passively in front of a television set watching other people live. Instead, they walk into a large empty room, the Holodeck, and immerse themselves in a computer-generated simulation of a situation. Sherlock Holmes' sitting room, Robin Hood's forest, Al Capone's Chicago, or future environments are all available to the crew of the *Enterprise.*

What does that have to do with your business trying to succeed? In order to change, you have to know where your company is going. Walking around in someone else's company gives a picture of *their* future and should be the foundation of discussion and planning and dreaming. But if people from your company could walk into an empty room and tell a computer to put them into the future of your company, what would they see? What would the company feel like? How would people behave? How would the work get done? What would management be doing? What would customers be doing?

You may not have a Holodeck at your disposal, but you may some day soon. In the meantime, you can refine the picture of the future in a variety of ways. One effective way is to set up a variety of scenarios that happen today and will happen in the future. Management looks at each of these scenarios, and each individual manager describes what he or she sees as the way the situation resolves itself in the future. In-depth depiction of specific situations and the comparison of future visions among the management group will bring to the surface areas of divergence that are minuscule today, but that will become major as the process continues.

Here are two examples of these "what-if" scenarios. You can design your own, addressing the critical issues that you want to see differently. The focus of this exercise is to do a reality check of management's individual and collective picture of the future. This is *not* the time to discuss either how to get where the company needs to go or the feasibility of trying to get there. This is the time to "blue sky" the company, to dream, and to remove the barriers to those dreams. When you are closer to the future defined by the vision statement on the wall, what would it look like from the perspective of the employee? Of the first-line supervisor? Of the CEO?

Worker Finds a Problem About To Happen

Louis had been uneasy for several days and he finally put his finger on the problem: the stamping machine on line #5. It did not sound right. He looked it over but could not see anything wrong. The machine had a heavy production run to get out this week to close out a big order. He patted the machine thoughtfully.

If this happened two years from now, what would you do if you were the

Plant Manager _____

_____

First-Line Supervisor _____

_____

Louis _____

_____

Continuous Improvement Is a Way of Life

" 'If it ain't broke, don't fix it' is my philosophy," growled Renee. "And, if it *is* broke, I'll figure out what to do about it. That's my job. That's why they pay me as a manager. People on the line don't really care anyway. They just put in their eight hours and go home." "No," countered Ken, Renee's supervisor. "It isn't going to be that way any more."

If this happened two years from now, what would you do if you were

Ken _____

_____

Renee _____

_____

Renee's Employees _____

_____

Once the vision/mission is defined and further refined at the senior levels, management needs to set up a system to cascade the process down through the organization. The forklift driver on third shift, the security guard in the most remote site, and the inventory clerk at corporate headquarters must all be able to understand what the vision means at their level. They need to enter the Holodeck to see themselves, their co-workers, their managers, their tools, and their location. They need to know how success is defined and rewarded, how decisions will be made, and how work will get done.

Then the change process can kick in. The present takes on meaning in juxtaposition to what the company wants to be, the future. The gap between the future and the present will drive the type and amount of change.

II. REAL WORLD   *Treetop Manufacturing Company*

CHARLIE

Charlie Kellerman has been the director of engineering services at Treetop Manufacturing Company for five years. He has been part of engineering services at Treetop for almost ten years. He moved to Lexington, Kentucky, to join Treetop from Detroit where he had worked as an engineer for General Automobile since he graduated from Purdue in 1969.

Treetop was founded in 1958. The company makes a variety of small appliances: microwaves, toasters, and irons. It sells direct to several major chains such as Wal-Mart and also sells to distribution companies throughout the United States and Europe. With sales of $500 million, Treetop has over 1,100 employees in three plants—two in the United States and one in Mexico—and a corporate office attached to the plant in Lexington.

Charlie has always liked working for Treetop, but lately he has been worried. He knows some of the new products their competitors have put out are pretty good. Worse yet, they seem to get their products into the market a lot faster than Treetop does. He has been doing a lot of reading and listening at conferences and workshops. He is convinced Treetop's engineering department could do a lot to improve their operations. So he was extremely pleased when John Shane, the president of Treetop, called him into his office and asked him to head up a special effort to improve the engineering process.

John has not been happy with the company's performance over the past two years. Sales have held, but profitability has slipped by over 12 percent and the market share is slipping. Marketing reports that there are great opportunities for growth in the Pacific Rim countries, but John is not sure the company is poised to take advantage of the potential growth and the quality demands that seem to come with doing business there. He has challenged Charlie and lots of other people to change so the company can recover what it has been losing and take advantage of new opportunities.

Charlie welcomed the assignment. He had begun to feel frustrated with his own career path. He was getting bored. Lately, there were no challenges. He was also nervous about John's orders. John sometimes shot from the hip. Charlie wasn't sure if John was really serious about all this change he wanted. What did John really want? How would Charlie know if he was meeting John's objectives?

Bored or not, Charlie wanted to keep this job. His family had settled nicely in Lexington. They liked it here, and the suburb they lived in was a great place to raise kids. Charlie knew the job market was good for engineers right now, but he really didn't like to think about changing jobs. His wife was talking about going back to school to get her degree so she could get a better job. She worked in the accounting department at a local dry cleaning business. She was bright and wanted to do more now that the kids were getting older. Charlie wanted to give her and the kids a few more years of stability before he thought about making any personal changes. Was this project going to put that hope in jeopardy?

Charlie quickly assembled a team of change agents, three of his best engineers, and settled down to the great task at hand. What was that task? It is one thing to want to make some changes. It is great to have senior management sponsor those changes, but now it got tough. What changes should they make? The team seemed to be going in circles.

Tom, one of the engineers on the team, was sure the problem was the suppliers. If they would deliver to spec and stop whining about over-engineered designs, manufacturing would not have a problem.

"We've just got to get tougher on those guys," Tom proclaimed. "We know how to design a good product, but everyone else seems to work against getting it built."

Charlie had to admit that Tom had a point. Just last month they had four major subassemblies so late they had to shut lines down. The suppliers were all trying to blame it on Charlie's department, but the components had been carefully designed to fit. If those suppliers would get smart, the future would be at hand!

Sam, one of the other team members, wasn't so sure. He wanted to examine the whole department and reengineer their approach to shorten the design cycle time. He'd read a book about reengineering and was sure that if they dismantled the department and started over from scratch, they would create a better and smoother operation than they had now. He kept talking about flowcharts and blank-paper thinking and how the way they were currently operating was clearly all wrong.

Jane, the third engineer on the team, said they should take one step at a time. There were a lot of things they could do. The first step was to do more studying. She wanted each member of the team to take a tool or a process that other engineering operations were using, like concurrent engineering or quality function deployment, and study it in depth. Then they would come back together, compare options and pick the right one to implement. But everyone knew what Jane really thought. She had said it many times over the past few months. She wanted the newest CAD system put out by the Pringer Company. She had seen it at a show last fall and was convinced she could deliver a major decrease in design time with this tool.

How was Charlie going to pick the right approach?

Three weeks later he thought maybe he had the answer. The office looked bleak on this cold, dark Saturday in February. Charlie looked at his watch. It was 1:00 in the afternoon. He wished he was at home. His favorite college basketball team was playing today, and he should be home watching. It was quiet here today, though. It was a good time to think.

Charlie had spent Tuesday and Wednesday of the week in Detroit. The Society of Manufacturing Engineers had sponsored a great session on engineering processes. Three major companies talked about how they developed concurrent engineering methodologies and what the payback had been. It was really exciting. Those companies were doing it!

John Shane was right. This company needed to make changes. Charlie was beginning to understand that Treetop not only needed to change, it needed to build the capability to continue to make changes, to take advantage of opportunities as they developed. From what the other companies reported at the seminar, the payback for making changes in engineering operations was substantial. They had learned some big lessons along the way about how to change, and one of the biggest paybacks was that they were open and receptive to more changes. They had made change a way of life for themselves. Those three companies had made serious strides in regaining a leadership position in their industries. Treetop could do the same thing!

Thursday morning Charlie assembled his team and reported on the seminar. This was a whole new way of thinking about building a product. The companies that had made presentations at the seminar had adopted a very rigorous methodology. They were stretching the use of their tools to the maximum and stretching their skills as well. They were highly disciplined, good at communicating with the nonengineering types. They seemed to have a clear idea what needed to be done and were doing it.

The team met his enthusiasm with a mixed response.

"See," said Jane, "I told you concurrent engineering was a good thing. Now if we just make sure we have the right tools to use, like that new CAD system, we'll be in good shape. We'll show John Shane we know how to make engineering really hum!"

"Wait a minute," said Sam. "Concurrent engineering doesn't work. My brother-in-law works for the Redline Engineering Consultants. They tried concurrent engineering and gave it up. If they couldn't make it work, we certainly won't be able to!"

Tom supported Charlie, barely. "It might be a good idea," Tom said tentatively. "If we bring our suppliers into the engineering process, it will give us a good chance to straighten them out. They're the ones who need to change, but I'm willing to set up a framework to get that message across to them. The easiest way would be to just put the fear of god in them, Change or Die, but if you want to go this route, Charlie, it's fine with me."

Charlie sighed. Were they right back where they had been?

Maybe not. He understood enough about concurrent engineering to see that Sam, Tom, and Jane all had some of the right ideas about change. Marketing had just reported that the average product life cycle was decreasing dramatically. That meant they had to get new products to market faster. John was pushing him hard to contribute to a major cost-reduction effort as well. Concurrent engineering could mean fewer engineering change orders in the product life. That might reduce the number of alterations manufacturing would have to make in its lines to get new products out.

These were all ambitious and worthwhile goals. What would it take to achieve them? Maybe the team needed to understand the change process. One of the things they had talked about at the seminar was that companies should not embark on a major change without knowing where they were going. Maybe the future was where they should start.

"Wait a minute, guys," he interrupted. "Let's not start taking steps to change until we've figured out what we want to change *to.*"

For the next four hours the team concentrated on where they were going. What would engineering look like in the future? What did a shortened design cycle look like? What did "shorter" mean? What kind of tools and technologies would they need? What skills would they have to have? What would be the role of management? As they struggled with these questions, the picture began to take shape. Treetop's engineering department was going to look different in a few years. As they finished for the day, they also agreed on something else. Treetop's engineering department was going to look *good* in a few years!

Charlie had spent most of this Saturday reviewing what they had done and putting the final touches on a report to John Shane. He was proud of what they had done. As he turned off his computer, he looked at his watch and realized the ball game would be over when he got home. His thoughts turned to his oldest son's request for a loan to buy his first car. Kevin was a good kid. He'd saved enough for the down payment on a car he'd fallen in love with. His job would cover the payments and the bank was willing to give him a loan if Charlie would co-sign. Maybe that's what he would do this afternoon—talk to Kevin about making the arrangements at the bank.

SARAH

As Charlie finally pulled out of the parking lot late that Saturday afternoon and turned toward the highway, he absentmindedly waved at Sarah Whitney. Sarah, equally absentminded, waved back. She too was lost in thought. Sarah had been with Treetop even longer than Charlie had. She had started out as a sales rep many years ago. Eventually she became sales manager for the toaster line. Two years ago she had been assigned directly to John Shane, in charge of strategic planning. Sarah learned her management style from the sales VP who was a slash-and-burn kind of guy. "Hit 'em hard," he'd taught her. "If they don't feel it they won't move!"

Sarah had been watching John over the past couple of years and learned that there was more to management than yelling and screaming at people. John could be impatient. He wasn't always clear about what he wanted, but he really seemed to care about people. Sarah watched him closely, trying to figure out how he managed.

Like Charlie, Sarah had had a meeting with John Shane a few weeks ago. He talked a lot about the problems Treetop was having and asked her to take

Figure 2.4
A Target for the Future

full-time responsibility for turning Treetop into an agile manufacturer. Sarah thought she knew what John meant by agile. She knew the operation had to become more flexible and *much* more responsive to customers. Treetop needed to improve quality, shorten cycle time, and reduce time to market.

She spent a few days after her meeting with John thinking hard about what had to be done. Then she turned on her voice mail, closed her office door, and powered up her PC. By the end of the week, she had sketched out a plan of action. The first thing she did was assemble the Agile Manufacturing Task Force. She picked an extremely diverse group of people, and their first charge was to create a picture of Treetop's future. They accomplished this task within a few weeks.

The task force picked a specific target to design their future around. That target was 100 percent on-time delivery of a 100 percent quality product with 100 percent customer satisfaction. A lofty goal. They painted a picture of that future and described it (Figure 2.4).

In Treetop's future the *processes* worked smoothly and delivered products on time. The products were designed for manufacturability. They were built right the first time so there were no rejects. Vendors delivered subassemblies and raw materials on time and perfectly made. Lines never went down. Raw materials got to them just in time. Preventative maintenance kept the lines running with no breakdowns. Capacity was maximized; bottlenecks were eased through.

Treetop's *structure* would look very different from the way it looked today. The team designed several configurations for how the company could look. They organized the company around products or processes. All of the options eliminated the current look of organizing around departments. On Sarah's organization chart, there were no departments of finance and information systems! The other thing missing on Sarah's chart was the current six layers of management. In fact, there was a *lot* less management.

People at Treetop were going to look different as well. Sarah had identified the skills that people would need in the future. Workers who made decisions, analyzed problems, and worked in teams needed different skills from those valued at Treetop today. Fewer people would be needed to get the current volume out the door. The types of people needed were different.

The *culture* of Treetop would not go unchanged. The future was a company where planning, not fire fighting, was valued; a company that defined what was expected of processes *and* of people, tracked the results, and rewarded people for achieving those results. Treetop would be a place where people were ready and eager to make suggestions, strive for improvements, focus on quality, and want to come to work!

What a great picture! When she and the team took that picture back to John Shane, he loved it. "This is great. This is what we need to look like. Now your job is to get us from here to there. You will not have to do it all, though. Charlie over in engineering will take care of his area. That is an area that needs a lot of change, but you don't have to worry about them. Charlie is a good man. He will deliver the changes that department will need to make. I would also like you to back away from the R&D group. They have a new manager, and I would like him to get his feet wet before we go marching in there and disrupt things. So leave him alone for a few months.

"While I'm thinking about it, I've had several conversations with the general manager of the South Bend plant. I know we have a lot of changes to make there, but I think you'll find him tough to work with. He is not very open to change, I'm afraid. I could replace him but I really don't want to do that. He only has a few years left until he retires. Let's see what you can do with his people while he is still there. Work around him.

"I'm a little concerned about our financial picture, too, Sarah. Why don't you lay out a budget and a time frame for me, and we'll go over the numbers together next week."

Sarah had been sitting at her desk all afternoon staring at her plan and thinking about her conversation with John. Now, a block away from the plant, she recalled waving to Charlie as she pulled out. What was Charlie's role now? Was he her partner? Was he her enemy? Was he a separate entity or an integral part of her success?

III. TOOLS FOR CHANGE

BUILDING A DESIGN FOR CONTINUOUS CHANGE

As the future becomes clarified, people throughout the cascade of the organization, from the president to the forklift driver, need constantly to question what the picture of the future looks like.

That future takes shape from four key perspectives: *process, structure, people,* and *culture.* While the final shape of the future keeps adjusting, the company needs to ask two key questions at the beginning of the process and keep asking those questions over and over again: (1) What will the company look like in the future? and (2) How will multiple changes complement or conflict with one another? Using the answers to these questions as a foundation, change agents can build a picture of the future.

1. What Will the Company Look Like in the Future?

What will be firm and fixed through time?

_____

_____

_____

What will be subject to on-going change?

_____

_____

_____

_____

What will be the same as it is now?

_____

_____

_____

What will be different?

_____

_____

_____

Describe the *processes* in the future.

_____

_____

_____

Describe the *structure* in the future.

_____

_____

_____

Describe the *people* in the future: their make up, their skills, and their interaction.

_____

_____

_____

Describe the *culture* in the future.

_____

_____

_____

How will people behave . . .

in their work group?

_____

_____

_____

with other work groups?

_____

_____

_____

with suppliers?

_____

_____

_____

with customers?

_____

_____

_____

with competitors?

_____

_____

_____

What will they believe is important . . .
in their work group?

_____

_____

_____

with other work groups?

_____

_____

_____

with suppliers?

_____

_____

_____

with customers?

_____

_____

_____

with competitors?

_____

_____

_____

2. How Will Multiple Changes Complement or Conflict with One Another?

Identify *all* major changes going on in the organization.

_____

_____

_____

Assess the relationship of these changes to one another and to the ultimate future of the company.

_____

_____

_____

Draw a fishbone diagram (like the one pictured below) to illustrate the changes and to validate that they are complementary.

Where are they in conflict? What is the impact of that conflict . . .

on the future?

_____

_____

_____

on achieving that future?

_____

_____

_____

3
Back to the Beginning —
The Present

THE WAY IT IS

"The way it is" can be described. A company can identify its current processes, operating structure, employee make up, and management style. It can define its culture in terms of people's behaviors, priorities, values, the rules they follow, and rules they break.

After a company or worker has been around for several years, describing the present gets harder and harder. People stop questioning inefficient use of resources, time, or people because it has "always" been that way. Much of what happens becomes so familiar that it becomes invisible. New hires are excellent guides to the present because their antennas are up. They are aware and watching, trying to understand the way things are.

Many change efforts, such as TQM and reengineering, have provided excellent techniques for defining the present. Those methodologies help you to compare where you are to where you are going and determine what to change and what to keep the same. But just looking at the current situation is *not* enough.

The people responsible for implementing change, the change agents, need to understand the present and its power to hold back change. The people who decide the organization has to change, the sponsors, also need to know the power of the way it is so their expectations for the change are reasonable. The people who have to change, the targets, are the ones who feel the power of the present state and need to break free of it.

WHAT IT IS TODAY

Current business literature highlights the role of the company's culture in changes. The organization's values drive its decisions and actions. Thus, those values result in a set of behaviors and processes that lay the framework for the day-to-day company activities.

The values that really drive the company are rarely the ones on the wall chart under the vision statement. The real values grew up over the lifespan of the organization and are seldom articulated, often out of ignorance and sometimes also out of shame. If the fundamental values of the organization did not see employees as partners, that value does not drive current behaviors unless the value has been systematically changed. If early values did not create win-win environments across functional lines, that is not the value driving organizational behaviors today.

When an organization looks closely at its values and their effect on current behavior, it describes its current culture. Some culture is written down. It might not be on a wall chart, but it is in the employee handbook, the procedure manual for requesting sick leave, or the documentation on how to run the punch press. Some elements of the culture are never expressed in a formal way, but they are reflected in performance reviews and conversations with co-workers:

- "If you want to know how to make our manager happy don't listen to what he says in the Monday morning meeting. Listen to what he yells about at his secretary on Wednesday. Then work on those items."
- "I know the production schedule calls for 500,000 of this item, but the customer always changes his mind at the last minute, so we usually run 7 to 800,000 and hide the rest in the 44th Street warehouse. Don't worry, it will get used up and the cost never gets charged to your account."
- "That stuff about happy employees all working toward a common goal . . . not here, and certainly not with the R&D group. Those guys will cut your throat every chance they get. Our job is to get them before they get us."

The culture of a company is as old as the company itself. It is an integral part of the company, defining the way it sees itself and the way others see it. Because it is deeply rooted and has its own set of rewards and punishments, formal and informal, it plays a major role in the outcome of the change efforts. Therefore, before beginning any change initiative it is critical to identify the current values, both at a global level and by department, operation, or location. Building a picture of those values results in a deeper understanding of current behaviors and rules and leads to a clearer picture of what has to change and what should remain the same.

Americans are fascinated with *British royalty,* almost as much as the British are. Americans create their own "royalty" by assigning that role to actors and singers. Media touts the reigning "queen" of the box office. While the nation's written values statements, in the Declaration of Independence and the Constitution, reject the concept of royalty and set up government without those roles, the people have assigned them anyway. The adoration, fascination, and disgust people exhibit shows that behavior and stated values are misaligned. The misalignment is showing up with government officials. The public tries to justify its fascination with the personal behavior of presidents, even though the stated values are concerned only with their ability to lead in their official capacity. It's more fun to examine the presidents' personal lives and behavior and speculate on what they are truly like, just as people do with Prince Charles and Princess Diana.

Many change initiatives die because people get mixed messages. They receive a rich pool of resources and tools to use to reach the future goals, but when there is serious trouble the message sent is: "Forget all that good stuff. Let's just get this problem solved. Our old tools have always worked for us in the past, so let's set aside the change effort and use the old way." That message reflects a value. Change is good, but only until we have a *real* problem. Then we rely on what has always worked.

It takes conscious effort to overcome the effect of culture. Even if you make some progress, details may mask your efforts. Forgetting to change language is one detail that can hide progress from senior management.

*M*oen *Inc.* was a long way into the future, but they didn't know it. When they ran into a major materials management problem and discovered that backorders on several major product lines were killing them, they announced that all their change efforts were on hold. They were going back to basics to solve this problem. The word went out—we will solve this problem the way we have always done things around here.

A close examination showed this was not true. The company was using many behaviors and processes that had been set up as a result of their new guiding principles to solve this problem. Highly effective teams developed quickly across functional and hierarchical lines. People were honest and open and did not hide their own responsibility and mistakes. Vendors were brought in and were treated as partners, working to solve a common problem, not as the enemy.

Communication about what was being done was open, direct, and frequent. Three years ago none of these behaviors would have been possible. It was a new culture taking shape, but it was using language left over from the old culture to describe the situation. The good news was the old culture was going away.

> The bad news was that the company had sent the wrong message to those who couldn't see what was going on. The company needed to correct its language.

WHY IT IS THE WAY IT IS

For successful change to happen, companies must not only examine the way it is today, but *why* things are that way. Assessing the present does not mean just taking a snapshot of it, flow charting a process, and examining the forms and procedures. It also means gaining an understanding of how things got to be that way. This understanding is critical to planning how to leave the present.

- How did things get to be this way?
  We always ran in lots of 100. That's the way the line was set up.
- How long have things been this way?
  Remember when we first started the deluxe-model steam-iron line? That was in 1985, and we built in the inspection process at each hand-off point because we were having so many quality problems with the crimp points during the first few months.
- What keeps things the way they are?
  Charlie from engineering complains a lot about this die and how long it takes to set it up, but the old plant manager used to work on this line. He never really saw any reason to change. After all, this line was one of our biggest and fastest producers. Why mess with success?

Things stay the same because the current way was successful in the past. Having experienced that success, people replicate behaviors that brought satisfaction, ease of execution, and a paycheck every week.

Today Is Grounded in the Past

The military model of running an organization has existed for thousands of years. Leaders do the thinking, planning, and decision making. They pass the responsibility for executing their decisions to the first lieutenant. That middle-management layer turns to the foot soldier and says, "March, fight, and, if necessary, die!"

It seemed logical to replicate that military model in American industry. Indeed, after World War II, many of the military leaders and the first lieutenants were recruited into industry. They took their way of viewing the world with them. There they found, in their companies, a pool of workers who had survived the fighting and returned home experienced in taking orders from the brass.

So the military model transferred itself into American industry, and it worked. Raw materials came to the back door. Goods were produced and went out the front door in exchange for a lot of money. Everyone was happy with the model.

Well, sometimes the soldiers wondered if there wasn't a better way to do things. They even thought about specific changes to improve things, but soldiers were not paid to think; they were paid to do. If they tried to change things, they were quickly shut down. The present way worked—why mess with it?

Many business writers, such as Peter Block and Michael Hammer, have written about how the present came to be. When companies started there were bills to pay and invoices to issue. As the volume of bills and invoices increased, it made sense to compartmentalize the work, create separate departments, and provide each with the forms and procedures they needed to do the work. Over the years, those departments, forms, and procedures became the way work was done. Therefore those departments and procedures became the way people defined themselves: "I'm in accounts payable." "I'm in production scheduling." "I'm from corporate accounting."

The systems did not always work well. Many people found themselves frustrated and annoyed because they were not operating at peak efficiency, but they blamed others: "If only those people on the loading dock would do their jobs, we would know when the materials came in and how much was left on the order. If they would do their jobs right, I could do mine!" Employees came to see themselves as operating very successfully. Even when the system did not work, it was some other department's fault. It was senior management's fault for not dealing with the other department.

In reality, it was everyone's fault. No way is perfect. All ways can be improved and enhanced at some point in their lifespans. Constant questioning of the status quo was not built into the system when it was designed. In fact, that kind of thinking was anathema to the military model; it was actually bred out of organizations. People who questioned the status quo, people who said, "what if . . ." or "how about . . ." were told to shut up and get back to work. Up until a few years ago, the business systems that evolved assumed that basic changes in the culture of the company were not necessary. Indeed, they were dangerous. Why tamper with a successful model?

So business solidified the status quo, and it worked for a long time. Now many companies, and even the military, have decided that a nonquestioning model does not work as well as other models. Therefore, they want to change something entrenched in the culture.

WHY IT STAYS THE WAY IT IS

The final step to evaluating the present is to understand how and why people stay there. This evaluation gives you clues to ways to help people move from the present toward the future. The present stays the present because it has great power to hold people. The future holds some fear, and the delta, the place where change happens, holds danger. Is it any wonder that people frequently choose not to change?

People are creatures of habit. When change becomes necessary people are often *victims* of habit. The status quo becomes second nature. You do not have to think about it. Driving to work the same way or taking the same bus or train to work every day frees you up to think about other things. You know the route. You know where to turn and on what corner to stand. Frequently people get to work with no conscious recollection of how they got there. Habits free people from the effort of planning, making decisions, paying attention to details, and thinking creatively.

Is this route the most efficient? Is it equally efficient every day? Would a different route be better on the way home? On Wednesdays? Maybe. It is easier *not* to change. Identifying the present and understanding how it came to be is important. It is also important to look at why the present persists. The tendency in managing change is to work from the logical—if you just examine the present and determine what parts of it do not work effectively anymore, you can then plan the change. "Logical," however, is a relative term. What appears to be common sense and logic to the change agent may be irrelevant to those who must change, because strong forces hold people in the present. The present keeps people back for three reasons:

1. The Present is Powerful.
2. The Future is Frightening.
3. The Delta is Dangerous.

1. The Power of the Present

The present is so powerful that at times it seems to defy logic. That causes problems for change agents. Change agents are often selected because they have common sense, an ability that management considers extremely important for effective change. That ability is a mixed blessing. People with common sense tend to expect the world and the people in it to behave logically. They frequently think that if they just show people the picture of the future, people will choose to go there because it is better than the present. Change agents get a lot of headaches, age fast, and often get beaten down by the changes they are trying to implement.

A manufacturing company in Maine has two plants located on the same campus as the corporate offices. In the office the clocks on the walls all reflect the time on people's watches, the same time as in the companies, schools, and stores around them; the time it really is. In the plants, the clocks on the wall are ten minutes faster than this "real" time. So when it is 10 A.M. in the rest of the world, it is 10:10 A.M. in the plants. Why? Many years ago there were a lot of complaints about traffic as people tried to get to work or home at the same time as everyone in companies near them. The company thought it would make sense to start and finish a few minutes earlier than everyone else in the area so people could get a head start on the traffic. That made sense, but people had trouble thinking about starting work at 7:20 instead of 7:30 in the morning and finishing at 3:20 instead of 3:30. They had always started at 7:30 and left at 3:30. It was too hard to change. So instead they changed the clocks!

Over the past few years, the company began to make changes in the way it operated: integrating more functions, creating problem solving teams that cross over department and location boundaries. It was hard to know when a meeting was supposed to start: now, ten minutes from now, or ten minutes ago! So it made sense to change the clocks back to "normal" in the errant plants, but nobody would allow that. This is the way it is. It has *always* been this way. Nobody but the change agent really wanted this change, even though everyone saw the logic of the request. It took two years of intense lobbying before the change agent got everyone back on the same clock, and then he had to cope with the original problem avoided many years ago. People had to come to work ten minutes early!

Language, attitudes, and feelings are part of what has to change.

Americans are changing the way they define the roles and responsibilities within the family. Fathers are playing an increasingly active role in day-to-day child care. Fathers and children are found in grocery stores, sports car road rallies, and gym classes. The behaviors, attitudes, and responsibilities of fathers have changed. So have their tools and resources. Diaper-changing tables are now found in men's washrooms almost as frequently as in women's.

However, some things don't change easily. Fathers who take full and complete responsibility for their share of the child rearing and nurturing hear people say, "How nice to see you baby sitting today." "Oh, are you baby sitting? Where is your wife?" The message implies that fathers and fifteen-year-old neighbor girls are in one special class, and mothers belong in another. The behaviors and attitudes have changed. The tools have changed, but the language has not. It still reflects an *old* behavior and an *old* attitude.

The present may not always be easy to explain or understand, but change agents should recognize that it has the following characteristics:

- It is comfortable.
- It is familiar.

- It works.
- It takes little energy.
- It defines people.
- It has a history.

Many people feel the present system does not work as well or make as much sense as it used to, but think they still do not have to change it. They just need to work harder at the present. Do it better. Do it faster. Then, everything will be all right. They do not have to change.

In his book, *Rethinking the Corporation,* Robert Tomasko calls defending the present "a vigorous fight to remain stable." In doing this the present becomes fragile and brittle and collapses.

> The present is so powerful that it frequently holds people long after it is gone. That is why few mergers or acquisitions provide the financial payback that appeared on paper. One company purchased a competitor about seven years ago. They kept the newly acquired company at arm's length, choosing not to assimilate it into the parent company. People often talked about the differences between the two companies. Those differences never really went away over seven years. Recently the parent company announced that it was going to divest itself of the subsidiary organization. Within 24 hours, people from the acquired company dug into their closets and their bottom desk drawers and pulled out their pencils, cups, jackets, and caps with the old company name on them. They displayed the old "present" proudly and rejoiced in its return. The old present never went away. The payback for both companies during those seven years of alliance was not as great as it could have been. The power of the past hindered success for both groups.

2. The Fear of the Future

While some people embrace change and others avoid it, everyone has to deal with the issues surrounding the future. Difficulty seeing and picturing the future creates the greatest issue. Also, the future pictured may not be desirable. If you are a first-line supervisor and one of the key elements of the future is an empowered workforce, you may suspect that there is no place for you in that future. You may not like the way the future is defined. Even as the present begins to look less and less satisfactory, it still holds us back. Its comfort and familiarity gain value as people look at the murky future.

The engineering department is frustrated with its other departmental relationships. Manufacturing complains about change orders coming too late or being too complex. For the past few years, information services has been on everyone's back demanding accurate, detailed information about bills of material and insisting on common part numbers for items issued from different factories.

While getting manufacturing and IS off their backs would be a real benefit, engineering may feel the price is too high. How much would engineering have to change? Why can't those other departments change and let engineering continue to do what it has always done? After all, hasn't that worked pretty effectively for many years? Too much change is not a good thing! From some of the things senior management is talking about, engineering might be totally reorganized. Some of the things they seem to want engineers to know and do sound like the things engineers *should not* be doing. It all sounds pretty scary!

3. The Dangers in the Delta

Change agents follow good change management strategies and spend a great deal of time defining the framework of the future as discussed in Chapter 2. Their common sense and logical approach then tells them they can sit back and wait for people to clamor for the change, but the silence is deafening! Why aren't people signing up?

Change agents must show people why the present is not working any more. They haul out charts showing the loss of market share and surveys of customers showing increasing dissatisfaction with the quality of the product. Surely people will now get on board. The future is great, and the present is not working.

However, there is another problem: the delta. Everyone has experience with change. They know what it is like. From that experience many people develop a dislike and discomfort with the third element in the change equation, the delta.

Leaving the comfort of the present is not easy. Moving toward a shadowy future is scary. Living in a place that is neither here nor there is hard. Struggling to operate in the new way runs the risk of failure. Management may decide that the change is taking too long, costing too much, or causing too much disruption, and then pull the plug on it. They blame change agents for the failure. People sometimes cannot learn the new skills, use the new tools, or behave in the new ways. They may find themselves being left behind.

All in all, the easiest thing to do is *not* to change. But companies that do not change die. Companies *must* change, and the good ones will manage the change to ease the pain, both to the company and the people.

CHARLIE

"This team is cooking!" thought Charlie as he watched Tom, Sam, and Jane, heads bent over an elaborate flowchart. They had been working on the chart all week, tracing the path of a design through the engineering department. After they fleshed out their picture of the department in the future, they realized the next step was to look at where they were today. So they papered the walls of the conference room with newsprint and began to track the design process.

The emerging picture looked like most engineering operations. They had never taken the time to develop a structured design methodology. Somehow it had just evolved over the years. There were lots of thick walls surrounding the department. They did not like the sales and marketing people and found the manufacturing people to be a pain. *They* just did not understand design. The focus of engineering's work was on the product. Naturally there were lots of specification changes through the life of the product. They constantly had to refine it and compensate for manufacturing's inability to make it right. Sales' lack of communication as to what the customer *really* needed did not help.

As the flowchart took shape, it was also becoming obvious that the present did *not* look a lot like the future. It was becoming clearer that there would have to be a lot of change if they were going to achieve the great future they had designed.

The project had been consuming the team for the past week. Charlie was fascinated to hear some of the team's conversations as they charted the path of a design product. Gradually, the story of the evolving development of the engineering department was told. Over the years, engineering had fought hard to win the respect of management and to get recognition for the role it played in Treetop's success. In the process, the department had been careful to protect itself from people trying to horn in on its expertise. A lot of walls had gone up, and a lot of steps in the production process had become duplicated, hidden, or omitted.

Something else emerged as the team talked among themselves and brought in other engineers to help them chart the work flow. People started talking a lot about what it meant to them to do the work the way they did.

Ken Willinger was one of those people. Ken had been an electrical engineer in the department for over 18 years. He sat at the same drafting table all that time. He had a great set-up. He was next to the biggest window in the office. He had made a special holder attached to his drafting table containing his ever-present coffee cup and a small plate for his morning danish, afternoon doughnut, and late-afternoon candy bar. When Ken came to Treetop 18 years ago, the department and the whole company was growing fast. There was a lot of confusion and wasted energy. Ken developed a procedure to track blueprints and designed a storage rack with a labeling system that worked very well. Everyone knew the procedure, and everyone knew where to find a blueprint, even one that had not been used for three or four years. Ken had made a comfortable world for himself.

A few months ago Charlie asked Ken to attend a workshop sponsored by the Association for Manufacturing Excellence. A company that had reengineered its operations conducted a discussion and tour for the participants showing what it had done and how it accomplished its successes. Ken reported that the conference was interesting, but he was not sure he liked what they were promoting. In that company, the entire engineering department was abolished. The engineers became part of the operational areas determined by product line. They served on teams with people from sales, from manufacturing, and even with the customers. The engineers who presented at the workshop talked about needing to know what the supplier's problems were, and how quality could be designed into the product. Ken agreed that all those things were important, but reported that this company had gone much *too* far and would be sorry in the long run. Charlie recognized that Ken, who had carved out a nice, comfortable, successful world for himself, was beginning to fear the future.

Charlie knew Ken was not the only person in the department who had made his life comfortable and familiar. He knew he had done it for himself. Large parts of his day had a routine that freed him from worrying about what he was supposed to do. While Charlie was pleased and excited by the work of his team, he was beginning to realize just *how much* change was coming out of all this effort. Charlie had never been particularly comfortable with change. In fact he worked hard to put structure into his life and give himself stability. His family laughed at his distrust of new things. His old car was clearly giving out, but he nursed it and spent hours under the hood every weekend getting one more week out of it. Kevin, his son, had a bright new car and teased his dad about parking next to "that old hunk of junk." Charlie didn't want to change. Charlie wondered if he was more like Ken than he would like to think. He had always known what to do. Now he was beginning to wonder if he was doing the *right* things!

The project team was doing some things right, though. They had a good working picture of the future. Now they had an excellent picture of the present. They were beginning to understand the power of the present, too, how it developed and why it worked in the past. That was going to help a lot as they figured out how to get from here to there, from the present to the future.

SARAH

Agile manufacturing. Sarah's team also was beginning to think they knew what that meant and how to achieve it. Like the engineering department, they were determining what to change by defining the present and comparing it to the future. They were also beginning to recognize why the present persisted. After all, Treetop had been around for a long time. The average length of employment at Treetop was 18 years. People stayed here. That meant the way things always got done was firmly entrenched. Questioning the way things were was not part of the culture here. Sarah remembered when she had first come into the corporate office as head of the strategic planning group. It had struck her as odd and not very smart that all the customer service reps went to lunch at the same time, putting their phones on voice mail. Why didn't they rotate and cover for one another? When she questioned the group, they laughed, "We've always done it that way, Sarah. It's the corporate way. You'll get used to it." She did not question it again.

Change did occur at Treetop. Procedures that were cumbersome or got in people's ways often were changed, but the changes were "workarounds" that developed informally. The procedure manual and the new-employee training still reflected the "official" way, but people found ways to defeat the system. They just didn't talk about them when the manager was around. If you were a new hire they didn't like, you might never find out about the "real" way to get work done. Making changes was not officially valued and rewarded. In fact, changing the rules was dangerous, even if it made the work flow better.

Sarah noticed an interesting phenomenon in the last few weeks. When people encountered her, they made sure she was aware of how hard it was to change. At lunch yesterday she joined the materials management group. They used the whole lunch hour to quiz her about the future. Was it really clear? Did it mean, as rumors were abounding, that materials management would be dissolved and the functions spread out into the plants? Were people going to get training in new systems and new functions? How serious was senior management about all this change? Was management willing to hang in there for the long haul this time or would they quickly lose interest, as they had done with the Just In Time effort?

Everywhere Sarah went she was getting these kinds of questions. As people heard about the potential for change, they were already looking at the present, what they knew about the future, and what they thought about the delta. They were already making decisions about whether they wanted to stay or go! There was a subtle but real wall going up around Sarah. She could feel it. People were beginning to recognize her as a change agent, and they feared the changes.

Sarah was beginning to feel uncomfortable and worried. How would she ever make change happen if she was isolated and feared? What would this do to her career at Treetop? Sarah had always prided herself on being well liked. Was this job going to drive her out of Treetop because people saw her as a threat to their existence? Sarah disliked the idea of not being liked or respected. She knew it would limit her ability to deliver these changes. A hammer approach to these changes clearly would not work. Her personal creditability and respect were on the line. Yet they were an asset she could use to manage these changes well.

Another major problem was beginning to surface as she and the task force went about the process of describing and analyzing the present. John Shane had put some constraints on her when he handed this project off. He had said Charlie Kellerman would handle changes in the engineering department. He had also said to leave the South Bend plant and the R&D department alone.

At the time, Sarah had been glad to hear those directives. She knew she still had plenty to do without those areas and was glad they did not fall under her responsibility. Now she was not so sure. Not being able to deal with these three areas might prove to be a problem.

One major aspect of the future of the agile manufacturing operation would be the ability to deliver orders to customers on time. The present state of that customer need was in pretty bad shape at Treetop. The Agile Manufacturing Team had collected data over the past 12 months, indicating that promised delivery was missed over 63 percent of the time. Worse yet, the biggest misses had been with their top two customers. Clearly, this was an area that needed change.

Sarah's group tracked the flow of an order to study the current process. They wanted to know where and how problems developed and caused those missed ship dates. They unearthed four major areas of concern:

1. *Quality problems with in-coming raw materials.* The materials were ordered with the required lead time from the vendors, but too often when they came in (on time) there were so many quality problems that large percentages of the materials had to be shipped back. This was happening primarily in the South Bend plant.
2. *Engineering change orders.* The number of ECO's was high, according to companies she had benchmarked. Equally important, the way they came out of engineering was causing a time delay. The ECO's went through three different paths before they landed on the desk of the foreman in charge of that particular operation. This process could take up to two weeks.

3. *Sales promising the world.* Sales reps received their commissions from the sales, not the level of customer satisfaction. So they did whatever it took to get the sale. Frequently, that meant making delivery date promises that were impossible to achieve. They knew those dates were not realistic, but they figured that was not *their* problem. Let production worry. If production screwed up, the customer service folks would calm the customer down. That is what they were paid to do!

4. *Products and subassemblies not designed for manufacturability.* Engineering never worked closely with manufacturing. They had tried, but cooperation between the two areas had never worked well. Manufacturing had learned to compensate. They prided themselves on their flexibility, their ability to modify lines and machines, to gerry-rig operations or the blueprints so the product could get built. This took a lot of time and energy. In many cases it had created quality problems that did not get caught until the cycle was in full swing.

Sarah was beginning to see the problems in the present. The problems seemed to fall into four categories: *process, structure, people,* and the Treetop *culture.*

Her team pointed out another issue that was a real source of worry. How do you make the changes to achieve an agile manufacturing environment without integrating *all* the changes required into one master plan? What was Charlie doing over in engineering? Would his change efforts help her achieve a future of on-time delivery? Would his change effort hinder her project? What about the general manager in South Bend? What was he doing about his vendor problem? Was he doing *anything* about his vendor problem?

She wondered if John Shane understood the repercussions of his directive. He might be setting her and Treetop up for failure if he kept walls around the various company changes.

III. TOOLS FOR CHANGE

THE WAY IT IS
Define the Present

There are excellent tools and techniques available to define the present; identify the work flow; align responsibilities; and measure current levels of productivity, quality, inventory turns, time to market, etc. The change agent must determine what measurements to use and set up a system for capturing those data.

Whatever approach you use, make sure the system identifies the present from these four key perspectives:

1. Process
2. Structure
3. People
4. Culture

WHY IT IS THE WAY IT IS
Trace the Development of the Way Things Are Today

Identifying the elements of the present should include a study of the organization's history. To systematically determine what to change and what not to change, change agents need to understand the origins of the present. The reasons for current procedures impact the ease or difficulty of changing and/or continuing with them.

How did the present get to be this way?

How did specific processes evolve?

_____

_____

How did specific structures evolve?

_____

_____

How did the current way of dealing with people evolve?

_____

_____

Where did our current beliefs and values come from?

_____

_____

What are the sources of the rules we follow?

Procedures and Policies

_____

_____

The "way things *really* get done around here"

_____

_____

Analyze the Power of the Present

Think about the people in your organization, your department, and the group targeted to change. What keeps them doing the things they do? Circle the number in the right-hand column that represents how strongly you agree with the statement in the left-hand column. The lower the number, the less you agree with the statement; the higher the number, the more you agree.

	No				Yes
People are comfortable with the way the work gets done.	1	2	3	4	5
People know how to do the work.	1	2	3	4	5
People are satisfied with the results of the way they currently operate.	1	2	3	4	5
People have developed a system for doing the work that takes minimal energy.	1	2	3	4	5
Our organization defines people by the work they do or the title they hold. Certain jobs and titles carry more prestige than others.	1	2	3	4	5
The way work gets done makes sense to those doing it.	1	2	3	4	5
The way work gets done does not always make sense, but people know it used to make sense and worry that maybe they are not doing it right.	1	2	3	4	5
Total Score					

The answers to these questions and others like them are the foundation for an implementation plan. The higher the score, the more entrenched the present is. The more entrenched, the harder it will be to change. Knowing this up front and analyzing the reasons for it will be the foundation for a change implementation plan. The answers will drive your communication efforts about the change and the change process. Training requirements are grounded in what people know now and what they need to know. The required adjustments in rewards and recognitions become apparent from this analysis.

4
The Great Chasm —
The Delta

CHAOS IN THE DELTA

Change is risky. People have to cope with the fuzzy, shifting future and the present's strong hold. If they do decide to change, they have to deal with the great chasm—the delta.

Change, especially complex, company-wide change does not happen overnight. The company travels from present to future through a period of time that is no longer the old way, but not yet the new way. The delta is where change occurs. It is where people stop operating in the old way, learn new ways, make mistakes, mourn the loss of the old, and test the new way. The delta is a limbo.

Because the future is a constantly moving target, a goal that keeps moving forward, the company needs to get comfortable with the delta. The future will never be a fixed place in time, closed to opportunity. You will always find yourself in a delta: a place where nothing is firm forever, a place of constant tension between stability and chaos, with chaos being the predominant force. Learning to tolerate this world is essential to your company's future. Within the delta ideas flare up, new directions develop, and chaos occurs. You cannot make the chaos go away, but you can learn to manage it. If you do not manage the delta, it will become a great void that will swallow you and your company.

Remember those 400 engineers in Dallas who tried quality circles? Why don't they have quality circles today? It was a very positive future. People certainly could have given up the present to achieve it. Quality circles died in a delta that was not managed.

Many factors make living within the delta hard:

- The delta is not the old way *or* the new way.
- The delta is not safe.
- The delta is expensive.
- The delta is sad.
- The delta is exciting.
- The delta is stressful.

The Delta Is Not the Old Way or the New Way

People do not know what is expected of them in the delta. They do not know how to behave. On Tuesday, they wish this whole change thing would go away and they could go back to the old way. On Wednesday, they wish they could speed the process up and get moving so the new way would get here. The delta is too long, too short, or both. This is very confusing to change agents who thought they had everyone lined up and ready for the change. Last night, when they left the office, everyone was enthusiastic and excited about their progress. Today, when they walk down the halls, they see long faces and signs of disenchantment everywhere. What happened? The delta.

The Delta Is Not Safe

The delta is where people learn how to operate in the new way. Learning often means trying and failing. Sometimes that makes people uncomfortable. Companies often reinforce that discomfort by making it tough for people when they fail: "Whatever you do during this change, make sure it is transparent to the customer." "You had better learn this new system because we won't have time to repeat the training." "We don't have much time to change so get it right the first time."

The delta is also dangerous for the people responsible for deciding what changes to make, the sponsors. In major, transformational change, even the most senior sponsors are also targets of change. They must change as well. If that change means losing power or behaving in unfamiliar or undesirable ways, they will resist the change.

*C*hina's leadership is a classic example of a group of sponsors who recognize that change is inevitable. Television, portable computers, and fax machines have opened their country much faster than any invasion by plane or gunboat.

However, they recognize that the changes required to interact as a major world player mean major changes for senior leadership. Their resistance to those changes is seen in the violence of Tiananmen Square and the tight controls over the timeline and process of the inevitable changes. Companies who want to do business with China must understand the leadership's reluctance to change themselves and watch how their resistance is exhibited.

The Delta Is Expensive

The bulk of the change dollars are spent in the delta. This is where the major communication and training efforts will occur. This is where the old and the new frequently overlap. New systems and processes may run side by side with old, eating up dollars: "We really should buy everyone who is staying late every night a pizza once in a while, but we don't have the budget for it." "We can't send anyone to any more conferences or seminars about how or what to change. We can't afford it. We have to conserve our resources for the change."

In a cavernous room at *Johnson Space Center* outside of Houston, scientists and engineers are building the components of a space station. This station should already be a viable, working laboratory in space. However, the next step in the changes that will lead to full space exploration is stalled for lack of funds. That lack of funds comes from the country's unwillingness to support further space exploration. The reasons cause agony for NASA and miles of speculation from newspaper and magazine columnists. Whatever the specific reasons, the bottom line is that the delta is too expensive and the public has slowed the change down. It will speed up again if and when the future state becomes more attractive and/or the present state becomes less palatable. Then funding will surge and a space station will circle the planet.

The Delta Is Sad

The old way worked. It may not have been the best, but it got the job done. In the process, it became familiar and comfortable. Leaving the familiar is sad, even when the future is exciting and positive. There is a feeling of loss for the way it was. You will probably never use a slide rule again, but you may remember using it, with amusement at its primitiveness and nostalgia for the memories it brings back.

*H*elene Curtis Industries knows how to deal with this sadness. They ritualized it a few years ago when installing a new manufacturing system. On the day the new system was to go into operation, three members of the project team showed up for work wearing tuxedos. They carried a small coffin and a portable tape player. They formed a solemn procession, carrying the coffin with reverence and playing the funeral march softly on the tape player. People snickered and laughed as they marched through the halls asking people to put something from the "old" way into the coffin, but everyone was curious as well. They followed the pallbearers and soon the procession grew. No one was laughing when the procession got to Nick's desk. Nick had designed a process years ago to speed up the information flow between sales and manufacturing. People had always valued that process and Nick's contribution. Now that process was going away, and as Nick put the forms and procedure manual for the *old* process into the coffin, the group became very quiet.

The pallbearers and their entourage marched out to the parking lot with the full coffin. Still in solemn demeanor, they put the coffin in a hole dug earlier. They buried that coffin, with dignity and honor, with humor and sadness. Then they turned off the tape playing the funeral march. They put in a new tape, a strong jazz sound full of joy and hope. They led everyone back into the office where the senior management was waiting to serve everyone a celebratory lunch.

The Delta Is Exciting

Unless they are brain dead, everyone has thought about how things could be changed: how work could be made better, easier, more productive, or more profitable. The delta is where those changes begin to happen. There is energy in the delta. People get a chance to try out ideas and test their skills, wits, and creativity. In the delta they see their ideas taking shape. Things they have longed for become reality.

Dave had worked on the assembly line at *Continental Cans Food Division* for over 27 years. He tried being a supervisor once, but asked to be relieved of the job after a year. It was not for him. Dave attended a seminar several years ago with about 40 of his peers, shop people going through major change. Dave described the changes the company was trying to make to be more competitive. They were creating a place where workers were respected, where they had a chance to give input, and help make things better. "All these years, if I saw a problem on the line and signaled for help, I had a bunch of guys in white shirts with pencils in their pockets come running over. 'What the hell's wrong?' they would yell at me. They made me feel stupid and small. Today, if I see something wrong or about to go wrong, I'll signal for help. A bunch of guys come running over, and they still yell, 'What the hell's wrong?' Then they say, 'This is your machine. You know it best. How can we help you?'"

As Dave told that story, tears came into his eyes. He quickly blinked them back, but everyone in the room saw them. Everyone in the room knew what Dave was feeling. The company still had a long way to go, but there was a lot of excitement in the group about what it was doing!

The Delta Is Stressful

With so many concurrent changes and the need to stay in business *while* the company changes, there will never be enough resources. There will never be enough time or enough money to hire all the needed consultants. There will never be enough people inside with the right knowledge and training. This lack of sufficient resources creates stress.

The security and ease of the old way disappears. People have to live in this complex delta as a permanent condition. The stresses that accompany the delta also become a permanent condition. Stress piles up at work as support systems fail.

Family support systems to handle stress are reduced as well. The spouse is coping with his or her own stress from a company delta. The extended family used to pitch in to help with child care, painting the outside of the house in the summer, and an invitation to dinner on Sunday afternoon, when everyone could all sit around and complain about how hard their jobs were. But now the family has scattered across the country. Those few who still live in the area are so tied up working overtime, nights, and weekends implementing change in *their* companies that they don't have time for family events.

> The belt division plant of *Gates Rubber Company* in Siloam Springs, Arkansas, has done a great job changing. Over a four-year period, they installed self-managed work teams. They reduced the number of support personnel (what most companies call management) from 81 to 78, while increasing the workforce by 100 percent. At the same time, they reduced the nonconformity percentage by 45 percent. It was not easy. Halfway through the change, Burt Hoefs, the plant manager, got a call from the local doctor. He informed Burt that the first-line supervisors were coming to him complaining of stress-related illnesses. As the number of supervisors decreased and people in the teams tried to take more responsibility, the supervisors found themselves working harder, trying to develop their new roles, to build the skills required to work with teams, and to help the workers to move through their own transitions. Physically, it was taking its toll.
>
> Burt understands how to manage change. He knew even before the doctor called that people were feeling the stress. He worked hard to diminish the stress. Where he could not do that, he provided help to cope with the stress.

NATURAL SELECTION OR MANAGED CHANGE

Some people like the challenge of change. They relish the delta with its confusion and risk. Others will do anything—even die—in order to avoid it. A character in Wallace Stegner's *Angle of Repose*, when moving to a new house, said,

"It is easier to die than to move. At least for the Other Side, you don't need trunks."

Unfortunately, companies cannot let a natural sorting process of who wants to change and who wants to stay behind be the criterion by which they change. You cannot let some people, who do not like the future or fear the delta, choose to stay in the present. The present is *going away*! It will not exist any more. The state of constant tension between stability and chaos in the delta is where people will live for the rest of their work lives. Therefore they need to understand the delta. Some people relish its challenge while others fear its existence. What makes the difference? Through change management, people can manage the delta, reduce the risk, and minimize the pain of moving through this chasm.

BRIDGING THE CHASM

Karl Wallenda of the Flying Wallenda family lived in the delta. His whole professional life was spent enhancing his skill at balancing on a wire high above the ground. His world was not the platform he started from, the present, nor was it the platform he got to, the future. His world was a 3/4-inch-thick steel wire suspended 10 to 100 feet off the ground.

"Hey, Mr. Wallenda, you gonna do the dangerous one tonight?"

"They're all dangerous," said Wallenda. His ability to live with the fear, excitement, and stress was his success. "Certainly we're afraid, but you must always feel safe up there. If you don't feel afraid, too, either you're a fool or you haven't got enough experience. You don't want anyone up there who is not afraid. You have to realize there is danger in front of and behind you. Don't get careless; don't get too tense. You can't go too far in either direction."

Constantly striving to develop his skills and knowledge of how to live in the delta is what made Karl Wallenda great. He passed that ability, those skills and knowledge on to his family who continue to live in the delta today. Karl died in the delta. He died an old man, choosing where to live and how to die.

A risk taker not satisfied with the status quo recently made a change. He climbed out of a hot air balloon (the present) and walked a plank (the delta) to another hot air balloon about twenty yards away (the future). This change was risky because the two balloons were 11,000 feet in the air! Was the delta risky? Well, how willing would you be to walk that plank (Figure 4.1)?

That is not a frivolous question. When you can understand why this man chose to take that risk and what drove Karl Wallenda to live on that wire, you can

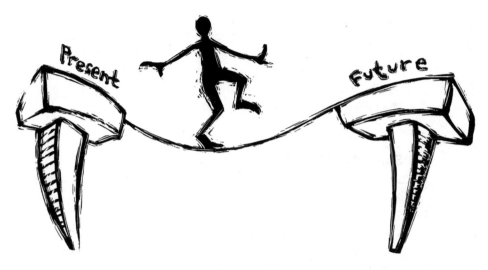

Figure 4.1
A Risk Taker's Walk

understand how to help your employees with the changes they need to make. When you understand why you would or would not take that risk, you understand how to help yourself through change.

Karl Wallenda and the man walking the plank 11,000 feet up in the air tell us a lot about change. They were willing to live in the delta. They used tools to survive: balancing poles, parachutes, and bungee cords. They were masters of balance in the delta. *Balance* is a key word.

Because the present is powerful, as you read in Chapter 3, it has a tendency to hold people, to keep them from stepping off onto the high wire. When a person or a company's present performance is good, or when change would be nice but is not necessary, the balance is in favor of the present. The future is always hard to see, with some positive elements and some things that people don't expect to like. The delta has many negative elements to it. Anyone asked to leave the present state and move into the delta does some quick assessments. Today is pretty positive, tomorrow is gray and fuzzy, and the future is a fast-moving target far away. It is not surprising that many people conclude that they will stay right where they are.

The present is successful, or at least it used to be. The future might be even more successful. But even if changing would improve things like customer satisfaction, profitability, quality, and time to market, going through the delta is a high price to pay. For many, not changing is easier because the balance works in favor of the present.

If you want change to happen, you have to alter the balance. You must minimize the negative elements of the delta. The pain of changing must be reduced. You need to give people balancing poles, parachutes or, at the least, bungee cords. At the same time, you need to eliminate the positive things keeping the company in the present by putting them in the future or just taking them away. The present must lose its power to hold people.

SHIFTING THE BALANCE

People and companies have to change when the balance shifts. When the present state is no longer desired people have to move. They change because the future is more desirable. That's how change happens. But the present state is a powerful force that tries to hold us in place. Every company experiences the tension between the stability and security of the present state and the need to make things better, easier, cheaper, and so on. When the stability and security of today result in success, there is little reason to change. The present is positive. The future might be even better, but why take that chance? What if it isn't, or what if it is too hard to get there (see Figure 4.2)?

Today				
Present	+	Delta	−	Future+/−

Figure 4.2
Today's Balance

In order to move people into the delta, the present must become less positive. Stability and security must become negatives rather than positives. That is not enough for change to begin, however. As you have seen, people often tend to stay in an undesirable present state if they do not see that the future is more positive and that the delta is survivable.

The job of the change agents is to alter that balance so that the present, the future, and the delta shift their balance (Figure 4.3).

Tomorrow				
Present	−	Delta	0	Future +

Figure 4.3
Tomorrow's Balance

From Stability to Chaos

Changing the balance means finding what it is about the present that no longer works or does not work well enough. Something is pushing on the present, forcing it to disintegrate so the company can move on to the future.

The impelling forces that create dissatisfaction with the present come from two sources:

- Outside the organization
- Inside the organization

From the Outside

Changes in customer demands are a strong change driver. Customers demand better quality. They say not to deliver product until *they* need it, but then they want it yesterday. They want to be your partner, but put very tight demands on what they expect from a partner.

If you cannot meet those demands, your competitors will. If you do not or cannot change fast enough, you can watch your competitors change and zoom right past you.

The use of information technology has created an environment where competitors can squeeze you and customers can demand more. Accessibility and depth of information are improving dramatically. This technological explosion is a tool and a force for change.

The world in which your company operates is also changing. Other countries are constantly changing, as are their industries. This opens up incredible new markets *and* competition. The changing world also means new requirements from governments, yours and others, and new environmental demands.

From the Inside

The way companies exist has evolved over time. Few organizations have consciously designed their evolution. During the past ten years, many people have begun to question the basic company structure. Companies have challenged the military model on which they were founded. Even the military is making vast changes. Within the army, air force, and navy are outstanding examples of well-implemented, positive changes. Many companies have changed their operations and dramatically increased their bottom lines. Companies in other countries operate in very different ways and are very successful; their success is threatening our very existence. So you may well wonder if your company should change.

There are many reasons to question whether the model that worked for so long can continue to work. Companies used to take what worked and do more and more of it. If specialization and compartmentalization worked on a small scale, they broke it down even further. If the data entry process initially meant all vouchers were entered on the fifth of every month, the department gradually got to the point where the address of the vendors was entered by clerk A, the amount (after several layers of verification) was entered by clerk B, and the approval to pay was entered by the supervisor. The process kept getting refined until it was very finite in each of its parts.

Today most people realize that companies have ignored an important potential pool of ideas, observations, suggestions, improvements, and criticisms. The nature of the old structure did not encourage workers to contribute. In companies that have overturned that present, workers are a rich source of improvements and changes, taking those companies closer to the future.

In that same vein, there is a much richer mix of workers in the workforce; more women and minorities are found in the total worker pool and in the managerial ranks. They bring to their jobs and companies different perspectives and different ways of thinking about work. Often they push against a model that workers in the past had accepted as inevitable and unchanging.

While technology has affected outside forces, it also affects the workforce within the company. Information is a source of power and control. In the military, secrecy and the "need-to-know" mentality are critical. That thinking transferred to companies. Management knew. Management told workers what management felt they needed to know. The power to keep or disburse knowledge was not hard to maintain because information flowed from disconnected sources that coalesced at the manager's desk. The manager had the control point.

With the onset of newer information management systems, the system itself becomes the information integrator and sorter. The system can easily channel that information to the right source at the right time. Management no longer *owns* information.

There are forces that have an impact on the present, making it less and less successful. People need to understand all of these forces. They need to see that while the old way, the present, has to go away, there *is* a picture of the future and, equally important, a plan to help them get through the delta. They need to *see* the bungee cords! With an understanding of the change process, you can put those balancing poles and bungee cords in place.

II. REAL WORLD   *Treetop Manufacturing Company*

CHARLIE

Sam was becoming a good change agent. As a member of the Engineering Improvement Task Force (the new name for the group Charlie had assembled), Sam had shown from the start an awareness of the need to pay attention to people, not just process. Today the team was meeting to plan a presentation for president John Shane on the work they had done so far.

"We're not ready yet," Sam challenged the team. "We're developing a pretty good picture of where we want to go. The walls in this room are covered with a flowchart showing where we are, but I'm concerned about how we're going to get people from here to there. How do we show people why they have to change? How will we help them to change? Why would they want to change? What's in it for them? We need to show John that we not only know where we're going and where we're coming from. We need to show him we know how to get there."

The team set aside their agenda for the day and concentrated on Sam's questions. Tom acted as scribe, writing a series of questions on the flipchart.

The Present

- Why do people stay here?
- What are the rewards here?
   The formal rewards?
   The informal rewards?
- What logical things hold them here?
- What illogical things hold them here?
- What still works well here?
- What does not work as well as it did in the past?
- What will happen if we continue to stay here?

The Delta

- What would make people feel insecure or scared?
- What would drain company resources?
- What would make people feel sad?
- What would make people excited?
- What would make people feel stressed?

The Future

- Why would people want to be here?
- Why would people not want to be here?

After they had listed all the questions, they went back and answered each one. Surveying the newsprint pages now pasted across the one free wall, Tom made an interesting observation: "These questions and their answers give us a path to the change. If we pay careful attention to what we have just done, we have the beginning of a change strategy."

Charlie kept thinking about Ken Willinger, his "stuck-in-the-old-way" engineer. If there was a chance to change Ken, it lay in the answers to these questions. While there were strong pulls toward the future—new systems, new ways of working with the rest of the company—there were greater pulls to stay in the present: comfort, ease, familiarity. He wondered if they really should change. How bad was the current situation? Did they really need to make such radical change? Was he the man for the job? Could he pull off this much change without totally destroying the department or maybe doing serious damage to the whole company? This thing was getting big, and it was getting pretty scary.

SARAH

On-time delivery was an excellent future to work toward, but Sarah had been wondering lately just how important it was. Her team's assessment had indicated that their current levels of delivery to promise were not very good, but were they causing any problems? Were customers unhappy? To find out, Sarah invited Ted Lamm, the vice president of marketing and sales, to lunch. What he had to tell her made her quickly lose her appetite.

"Sarah, we are in serious trouble. We are about to lose the Framingham account. They are our biggest customer! They claim they cannot work with us any more because we're not meeting their delivery specifications. They have also been complaining about the number of returns on the new steam iron we introduced last quarter. Framingham is 35 percent of our business. I don't know what we will do if we lose them!"

Sarah swallowed, the fear stuck in her throat, and asked, "How sure are you, Ted? Is there a chance they will change their minds?"

"I talked to the vice president of purchasing last night for an hour. He said they hate to cut us out, but unless they see evidence of real change from us, they're going to cut our shelf exposure in their stores by 65 percent and give it to our competitors. I told him I'd be back to him in three days and show him our plan for addressing his concerns. Do we have a plan, Sarah?"

"Well, I thought we did," Sarah said. "We know where we want to go. We've carefully mapped where we are today. There are a lot of plans taking shape to figure out how to get there: what tools to put in place, what changes to make, what to eliminate, what to add. But I have been pretty worried about whether or not people will be willing to change, whether they will tolerate all this change. Listening to you, Ted, it's clear there is really no choice. So I'm going to add to our plan. I'm going back to my office to think through how we help people get from here to there. Then you'll have that plan you need to show to Framingham!"

As she headed back to her office, she passed the engineering department. One of her task force members had heard that Charlie's group was spending a lot of time thinking about how to help people change. She should probably talk to him, but right now the most important thing was to put together an implementation plan.

III. TOOLS FOR CHANGE

ALTER THE BALANCE

The next step in the change process is to determine why the current balance is holding people in the status quo. Gather the necessary data to determine what can alter that balance, move people out of the present, through the delta, and toward the future. Use the questions Sam and the engineering department developed.

Today

Present	+	Delta	−	Future +/−

The Present

- Why do people stay here?

  _____

- What are the rewards here?

  _____

  The formal rewards?

  _____

The informal rewards?

_____

• What logical things hold them here?

_____

• What illogical things hold them here?

_____

• What still works well here?

_____

• What does not work as well as it did in the past?

_____

• What will happen if we continue to stay here?

_____

The Delta

• What would make people feel insecure or scared?

_____

• What would drain company resources?

_____

• What would make people feel sad?

_____

• What would make people excited?

_____

• What would make people feel stressed?

_____

The Future

• Why would people want to be here?

_____

• Why would people not want to be here?

_____

Tomorrow				
Present	—	Delta	0	Future +

MANAGE THE DELTA

Once people understand the cost of not changing, they may still be reluctant to change because the change process itself is so difficult. Change agents need to reduce that difficulty by putting in place the resources to help people move through the delta. Start by assessing what kind of resources are currently available and what you will have to develop. One key resource is the company's ability to live in a delta state. Use this questionnaire as a way to assess your delta tolerance.

The delta tolerates confusion.	**Yes**	**No**

Examples: Sponsors talk about the lack of a clear direction, explaining constantly the changing customer requirements, the confusion caused by the marketplace. They reinforce the point that deltas are never clear and crisp directions. They tell stories of their own shifting focus and false starts and stops.

The delta has a mourning process.	**Yes**	**No**

Examples: Whenever a symbol of the old way is removed, it is removed with honor and respect. Speeches, ceremonies, and celebrations become a way of life; some very formal and well planned, others spontaneous, even individual.

The delta has a learning process.	**Yes**	**No**

Examples: Targets see the delta as a place for acquiring new skills, gaining new understanding, and stretching their abilities and intellect. Time for training is not given begrudgingly. Senior management is seen actively learning along with the hourly workforce.

The delta can handle mistakes.	Yes	No

Examples: Stories of screw ups become part of the culture, but as stories of learning and experimenting, not of ruined careers and ulcers. People who try and fail are rewarded for trying and not punished for failing. These stories are told to new workers by the formal system and by workers over a cup of coffee.

The delta allows people to express their fears and concerns.	Yes	No

Examples: Meetings, surveys, focus groups, and coffee time allow open communication. Opinions and concerns are solicited by the formal structure such as the human resource department, but also informally through the management cascade. Feedback mechanisms to provide answers and allay fears are seen as a direct result of the input that targets have given management.

The delta provides people with resources to cope with stress.	Yes	No

Examples: The company sponsors employee-assistance programs, education in change management, three hours off on a Thursday afternoon to go to a baseball game, and family support such as information, counseling, and fun time.

PART TWO

The People Part of the Change Process

The greatest impediment to a successful change is not the amount of resistance from people who must change. Resistance can be managed and dealt with. Successful resistance management cannot happen, however, unless everyone knows their job in the change process and is prepared to accept their responsibilities. Clarifying those responsibilities and building the skills to carry them out are the most important factors in a successful change.

To gain control over the change process, you must answer some critical questions. Who owns the change? Who is supposed to implement the change? Who will the change have an impact on?

Sponsors set up an environment of change. Company management is the sponsor of change. They set the future's outside boundaries through the vision and mission and allocate resources to make changes happen. If they do a good job, they dramatically increase the chances for a successful change.

Sponsors turn to *change agents* to implement the change. Analyzing successful and unsuccessful changes helps you understand what change agents have to do. A set of skills is associated with being a change agent. The change agent's use of those skills has an impact on the success of the change.

Daryl Conner, in *Managing at the Speed of Change,* calls people who have to change *targets.* Many people protest that name, pointing out that it represents a passive object or person receiving pain. Change agents in companies going through a great deal of change verify that target is a very appropriate word in most change situations. In an optimal change environment, a target would become a partner. However, sponsors and change agents must work hard to make partners of the people who have to change. For ease of discussion, this book uses the term target. You will have to determine the most appropriate language for your company.

OVERLAP AND SCHIZOPHRENIA

Finding someone in any company today who is *not* a target of change would be nearly impossible. The complexity and rapidly moving nature of today's marketplace means that no one is immune to change. Therefore, sponsors and change agents are also targets of the very changes they order and deliver.

This is a very important point. The president of the Fortune 500 company and the vice president of the 25-person firm must change. The vice president of marketing and director of materials management must change. *No one can escape change today.* That is why it is critical to define the future as clearly as possible and clarify all kinds of changes that must happen in the delta. Without that clarity, it is easy to dismiss the need for change at the top and in the middle and to focus on the changes required by the workforce: new information systems, new departmental organizational structure, or a new work flow. This focus is not enough, however, to survive the delta and move toward the future. Management must change its thinking about the way people work together within departments and across department boundaries; about the way people are managed; and about the way they think about the business, about customers, about suppliers, about the people above them, and about the people below them.

Targets are found throughout the company, included in the sponsor ranks and among the change management task forces and implementation teams. Senior management is a key target of much essential change. A good change management plan recognizes this and addresses the needs of *all* targets, starting at the top of the organization. Unless this happens, senior management often appears schizophrenic, doing all the right things one day and seeming to run for cover the next. One day they feel like sponsors; the next day they feel like targets.

In this section, you will study each role in the change process and determine the needs and responsibilities of people in each role. Gaining control over the role of sponsors, change agents, and targets means gaining control over the change.

5
Sponsors of Change

The word *sponsor* has different meanings in different companies. As author Daryl Conner points out, a sponsor is someone who has the authority and responsibility to order a change. Until a few years ago, only people in management had that authority and responsibility. Today a few places have successfully pushed that responsibility and authority down into the workforce, and workers are their own sponsors within defined change boundaries.

> The Gates Rubber Company plant in Arkansas (considered in Chapter 4) has empowered their workforce. The people on the shop floor have the authority and the responsibility to sponsor changes within their sphere of influence. People in work cells are given weekly production goals by the customer. To achieve that weekly bucket of work, they have the authority and responsibility to change the production schedule, work schedules, handling of raw materials, and whether they work overtime or not. Most significant to sponsors and change agents is that the people on the shop floor asked for the change to this level of empowerment. Through their Opportunities for Improvement Communication System, they asked senior management to give them a higher level of sponsorship.

CHANGE FROM THE TOP OR FROM ANYWHERE

Many people debate the source and direction of change. Can the director of engineering and a few bright people in his or her department initiate a change? Can five or six engineers sitting around at lunch when the director is out of town initiate a change? Can the change come from the industrial engineer on the shop floor? The answer is yes *if* the sponsors above these people have given them the responsibility and authority to make changes. If not, there is no change. The picture is very simple. When the people above you in the organization have given you the authority and responsibility to make a specific change or to make changes within a specific parameter (no greater than $45,000 expenditure or only within the inventory control department), you can sponsor changes on your own. If that change sponsorship has not cascaded down, you are not a change agent. You are simply a person with a great idea!

The best sponsors make the greatest contribution to their company by delegating vast amounts of authority and responsibility. At the same time, they set tight limits on change and change process, open up the present state, and get out of the way. If they do not, change agents and targets will use the delta to experiment with ways to return to the present state or to design a future state outside the company's vision.

> **D**uring the early 90's, *Kraft FoodService, Inc.* had people initiating and implementing changes all over the division. Change seemed to sprout up and go into effect in pockets. It did not appear that change sponsorship was cascading down through the organization until you looked closely. The president of the food-service division had sponsored a change that empowered people throughout the division to initiate change. Without the president's sponsorship of that change in thinking, the pockets of change would not have survived. By empowering people in this way, the president set parameters for the changes. They must fit within the vision and contribute to the future. There are budgetary and overlap constraints, but change is a way of life. Empowerment to make change happen meant that Kraft FoodService was in constant change. It was a way of life the employees wanted to maintain and strengthen. They recognized that the delta is a permanent condition; there will be constant tension between the need to be stable and the need to change.

Authority and responsibility flow *down* through the organization. That has not changed, although there are fewer layers of management in many companies today, and those layers are organized by product or process. Many of those companies have passed that maturity and responsibility into matrix management structures. Sponsorship for change still comes from the top, but demanding change will not work. The cost of forcing change through the organization is high. Often the price is failure as people sabotage the change effort or return to the old way once the sponsor's back is turned. Effective change sponsorship is a special skill. It means rewriting management's job description.

A NEW JOB DESCRIPTION

Change sponsors rarely have the luxury to focus solely on that sponsorship. They have to fit sponsorship in along with everything else on their plate.

Sponsors must operate successfully in three key areas:

1. Sponsors understand the changes they are supporting.
2. Sponsors manage the resources required for change.
3. Sponsors deal with people involved in the change.

1. Sponsors understand the changes they are supporting.

Signing a vision statement is one thing. It is another thing to truly understand the depth and breadth of the changes authorized by that signature. What does "empowerment" mean? What truly is world-class manufacturing? What will the company be if we double our size in the next ten years?

Sponsors need a dialog with the organization to ensure that they know:

- The boundaries of the future.
- What is flexible about the future.
- What is inflexible about the future.
- Whether all the ongoing changes fit together and contribute to that future.
- What changes to make in structure, process, people, and culture.
- How much senior management and the managerial hierarchy will have to change.
- What impact the change process will have on the change.
- Forces of resistance that will be unleashed.
- What skills and abilities people will need to survive in the delta and strive for the future.

2. Sponsors manage the resources required for change.

Change costs money. Sponsors have to allocate the money required for change. They also need to understand the implications of not fully funding changes.

Change takes time. Sponsors must understand the implications of setting time fences for implementation and the impact of aggressive implementation schedules. That does not necessarily mean backing off from an aggressive schedule. It does mean having sufficient knowledge of the change process to know how a fast pace affects the planning process, the degree and type of resistance, and the problems of the delta.

Sponsors must support change agents involved in the changes. The change agents plan and implement the specifics of the changes. They need change management resources such as communication, learning, and rewards. They need to understand the change process. They need to be accountable for implementing the change. Supporting and developing change agents, helping them to get needed resources, and setting up a system of accountability are key sponsor responsibilities.

When a change moves through the delta, the organization's resources are seriously drained. While carrying on business as usual, the organization must simultaneously make changes happen. People need to learn new skills, practice a new way of working, experiment with altered tools, and refine the future as new information surfaces. This takes time. It means trying new things and often failing. It means using more resources than normal and taking great risks in the delta. Sponsors must decide how much resource drain the organization can tolerate and how many mistakes it can absorb.

3. Sponsors deal with people involved in the change.

No procedure changes without people changing. No new tool gets introduced without people changing. Change is all about people; the ability to deal with and work with people successfully is critical to a sponsor.

Sponsors must understand what will happen to people in a change. They must be empathetic to the pain of changing. They do not back off from difficult change because people are hurting, but they let people know they understand and will do whatever can be done to diminish that pain.

Sponsors must communicate. They must articulate the future and paint a picture that targets can see. They must be able to listen and hear people's fears, frustrations, excitement, and confusion.

Sponsors need to be risk takers, showing others they are willing to experiment in the delta, tolerate making mistakes, and look awkward or even foolish. They must accept the fact they do not know everything. People need to see them struggling to change in the delta.

Sponsors need to tolerate risk taking in others as well as in themselves. Living in the delta means almost continual risk, testing the changes, experimenting, modifying, and adjusting. Sponsors must become comfortable with others taking risks and must make people comfortable with risk and with failure. This is a skill set that most senior managers do not have today.

Sponsors must be intuitive about when to lead, when to work as partners with change agents and targets, and when to get out of the way. This is a critical skill. Knowing how to provide the right level of involvement means understanding people and the changes they are making.

Sponsors need to know how to coach, encourage, cheer, advise, and counsel people as they leave the present and bounce around in the delta.

Sponsors think they have to be passionate—and they do. If they do not believe in or care about the changes, they will have a hard time behaving as good sponsors. You can't fake it! Passion is frequently misunderstood, however. Many managers think they have to be brilliant and inspiring speakers, able to rouse the troops with their eloquence. That's nice, but it's not necessary. There are many ways sponsors can show that they really care.

> *Waterloo Industries* in Waterloo, Iowa, makes storage containers. One of their biggest products is the line of toolboxes they make for Sears. Several months ago I spent two days working with the management team. We met in the showroom where all their products are proudly displayed. I noticed something interesting every time we took a break and at lunch. John Trebel, the president of Waterloo, and everyone else in that group always gravitated over to those products. They talked about them, analyzed them, and touched them. They were always touching their products. They ran their hands over them, picked at the lids, and just let their hands rest on the boxes as they talked. Workers at Waterloo do not have to wonder if their management cares about the products, about whether they are made as well as they can be, or even better. They see management touching those products. That's passion!

DEFINE THE JOB

Building effective sponsorship starts with a definition of effective sponsorship. The following chart identifies the three key responsibilities of a sponsor. The specific behaviors required and the level of performance needed for that behavior is defined in the second column of the chart, "Targeted Performance."

Key Responsibility	Targeted Performance
Understand the Change	• Define the future as much as possible in both numerical and behavioral terms.
	• Gain consensus for the future down through the organizational structure.
	• Identify and communicate what is firm and nonnegotiable, and what is open to refinement and adjustment.
	• Show pictorially and operationally how this change fits into the framework of a larger change, and/or how the change integrates with all other changes going on in the company.

	• Define the changes required of management to achieve the future.
	• Show understanding of the impact of the current culture and the history of change in the company on this change effort.
	• Commit to dealing with the degree and type of resistance that will surface regarding this change.
Manage the Change Resources	• Allocate the dollars required for this change or explain why dollars are not available. If the dollars are not available, lower future expectations, provide alternative resources, or prepare for a less successful change.
	• Allocate time required for this change or explain why time is not available. If the needed time is not available, lower future expectations, provide alternative resources, or prepare for a less successful change.
	• Identify and empower effective change agents.
	• Make sure the required change management resources are available: 1. Communication System 2. Learning System 3. Reward and Reinforcement System
	• Identify the amount and type of loss tolerable in the delta: 1. Productivity 2. Customer Support 3. Profitability 4. Stress Levels
Deal with People	• Exhibit empathy and understanding of the difficulties of changing.
	• Communicate the future from the target's perspective, using the target's language.
	• Establish multiple listening opportunities to allow people to express resistance and fear.
	• Let people see that the sponsors are making changes and having difficulties.
	• Take risks and encourage others to take risks.
	• Provide a constant beacon of support and encouragement.
	• Coach sponsors, change agents, and targets to develop their skills in both the change process and the changed processes.

In the spring of 1994, when *South Africa* stood on the threshold of major change, *Nelson Mandela* and *Frederik W. de Klerk* were clearly sponsors of those changes. They were passionate, and they were visible. They were flexible in their leadership styles, and, most important, neither allowed the future to be defined in too great detail. They couldn't. They didn't know what it would look like, but they *did* put outside boundaries on it. They showed people that there would be a framework within which all the changes that were about to be unleashed would fit. Whether you liked that framework or not, you could see it. You saw it being painted by two men who had been locked in mortal combat all their lives, who were suddenly working together.

TARGETING SPONSORSHIP

Change sponsorship can be learned. Until now, people with the authority and responsibility to order change did not have many ways to learn what to do after they put in their order. They have struggled on their own to figure out what to do. Many of them failed. Those who succeeded have become the objects of study: Bob Galvin at Motorola, Jack Welch at General Electric. What did they do? How did they do it? Careful reading about these master sponsors does not ensure that others will be able to emulate them.

If you are not already a good sponsor of change, becoming one *is* a change, and change is hard. Just knowing what to do is not enough. Effective sponsors got that way on their own. They were targets, targets who had to change the way they sponsored change. You can help develop sponsors by teaching them to apply effective change management skills and behaviors.

Changing people into good sponsors means using a variety of techniques:

1. Show them what good sponsorship looks like. Lessons from Galvin or Welch are examples. They model what sponsors and change agents need to be. They *are* the future of sponsorship.
2. Show sponsors what today looks like. Use the chart above to educate sponsors. Assess their sponsorship level, and show the targets the gap between where they are today and where they need to be. Show them the forces pushing on them for better sponsorship—both external forces driving the changes and requiring success, and internal forces such as people's perception that sponsors are weak and the change is doomed to failure.
3. Systematically apply change management methods to improve the sponsor's sponsorship:
   • Communication system
   • Learning system
   • Reward/reinforcement system

Bill *Clinton* has had a problem with sponsorship. Shortly after taking office, Clinton and *Al Gore* made a big splash in the press with the extremely well executed announcement that they were going to streamline and reengineer the federal bureaucracy. They are trying, but below the cabinet level, an appointed office entirely dependent upon the current administration, is a cascade of federal managers who are entrenched by history and by the civil service system. Scattered throughout the federal bureaucracy are thousands of people who would like to change. Sitting at the top of the system is an administration that wants to change. Pushing from the outside are millions of citizens fed up with inefficiencies, poor customer service, and waste. Why don't things change? The sponsor cascade chooses not to change. They will neither change themselves nor will they sponsor changes down through the cascade. There are laudable exceptions. These exceptions must become the norm or the bureaucracy will continue.

II. REAL WORLD   *Treetop Manufacturing Company*

CHARLIE

Charlie has been thinking a lot about John Shane this week. John is the sponsor of Charlie's change. He authorized it and takes responsibility for it. Since Charlie's team has defined what they think the department should look like and assessed where they are, he is beginning to sense the enormity of the changes they need to make. The team is having those same thoughts.

"I guess our future in engineering is a lot more than a CAD system," Jane reflected today at their meeting. "The system is just a tool. The real changes are going to come from the way people think about the engineering tools and about engineering. When I say people, I mean more than just the engineers. Manufacturing, sales, even finance will deal with us differently in the future. Charlie, how do we make changes in engineering that require change in other departments? We don't have the authority to make changes in manufacturing. How are we going to succeed?"

Charlie knew John was the key. Back at his desk after the meeting, Charlie reached into his lower left hand drawer and pulled out Treetop's organization chart.

Who was going to be affected by their planned changes? Who would impact whether or not engineering was able to change? Manufacturing certainly was a key player. The changes engineering wanted to make meant manufacturing would have to change quite a bit. They would have to be part of the early design process. They would contribute as partners in design, not as adversaries

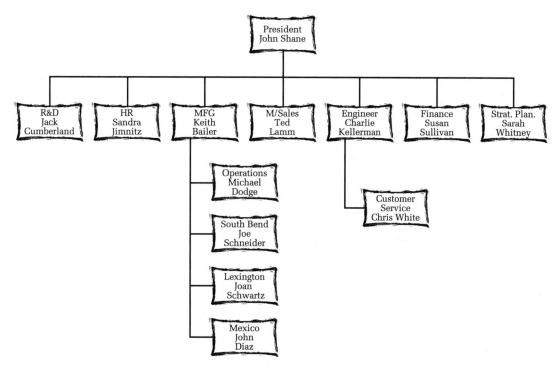

Figure 5.1
Treetop's Organization Chart

waiting for engineering to throw their designs over the fence. Did they have the skills, time, and inclination? Would they embrace this change or meet it with suspicion?

Would this chart itself change? Maybe those separate boxes identifying functions would go away. Charlie's group was beginning to understand that no department could change by itself.

If designs were converted into manufactured products with fewer problems and changes in dies, less struggle to achieve quality levels, and better raw materials coming in on time, manufacturing would think it had died and gone to heaven. But achieving their wishes would mean they had to change. Could they cope with these heaven-sent blessings? Did they have the tools to measure the established standards? Would they be able to supply the lines at a faster rate of production? Could they cope with the smaller lot sizes possible because of these improvements?

Keith Bailer, vice president of manufacturing, was a good man. Was he good enough to absorb all this change? He had been complaining for years about all these problems. Charlie thought Keith would probably welcome these changes, but would he know how to sponsor them? Charlie knew Keith had been having problems with Joe Schneider, the plant manager at South Bend. Joe was getting ready to retire. Joe's thinking was a lot different from Keith's. He had said many times in the last few years that he did not see what all this hoopla was about. If the company would just get back to basics, they would do just fine. They did not need a lot of fancy changes. People were basically just lazy and careless, and if you just stayed on top of them, you could run a really efficient operation. That is what Joe wanted to do until he retired: run a tighter ship.

Systematically, Charlie went through the rest of the organization chart. He identified the places where there would be a major change impact and deter-

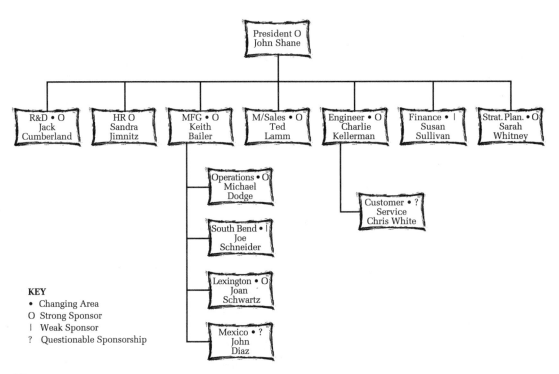

Figure 5.2
Sponsorship Strength

mined what kind of sponsorship he could get for change in those areas. When he was done, the organization chart was dotted with marks: stars for areas that would have to change, red circles for strong sponsors and yellow check marks next to the names of people who Charlie feared would not or could not sponsor the changes required. He put a question mark where he was not sure.

He was pleased that John Shane did *not* have a ⏐ next to his name. At least the senior leader was a good sponsor. At least he *meant* to be a good sponsor, but how good was he? Thoughtfully, Charlie changed from a circle to a question mark next to John's name. He smiled ruefully as he looked at the chart again. He had identified himself as a strong sponsor.

"I think I understand the changes we have to make," he thought to himself. "The future of the engineering department is taking shape and I think I have a sense of just how much and what kind of change that means. I am willing to step up to the fact that there will be resistance, and I think I'm beginning to understand how to deal with that. As for resources, that's a worry. I don't know how much time these changes will take and I don't know how much time we have. I certainly don't know how much all of this will cost. My team and I had better scope out costs. I guess we need to do some more thinking about implementation and lay out some plans. Maybe I need to check on my sponsor skills when it comes to people. I've been so focused on processes and systems; I wonder if I have the management skills to lead people through this delta *and* to manage in the future. I think I'll have a talk with Sandra Jimnitz in Human Resources.

"Looks like we've got our first change assignment, though. Starting with John, I had better take a close look at this sponsorship and make sure I've got what I need to carry off these changes," he murmured to himself. "But I know Sarah Whitney is making a lot of changes in these other departments. I wonder if she is going to get in my way or if maybe we can get together on these changes. Are they compatible or are they in conflict?"

SARAH

John Shane was mad. He was more than mad; he was livid. Sarah did not think she had ever seen him this angry. Ted Lamm had just told him about the Framingham account. "Sarah, this is exactly why I asked you to take on the job of fixing this place," he shouted. "What are we going to do if we lose this account? What have you and that task force been doing? If you can't do this job, we'd better get someone in here who can!"

"I'm working on it," Sarah explained. "We've got a good picture of where we need to be and where we are. The task force has developed a series of plans for closing the gap, John. We're putting the finishing touches on the implementation plan right now. I talked to Ted too. He assures me that if Framingham sees we are serious about changing and correcting the mistakes they've been seeing, they will give us another chance. I will have the final plan ready for you and Ted to see tomorrow morning. I am sure if Ted takes it to them, they will back off."

"Well, they better," growled John. "And you better have a good plan. More than that, you had better be sure you can pull this plan off, Sarah. All we are doing right now is buying time, but we must be able to deliver."

Sarah did not exactly skip down the hall to her office. When she got back to her desk, her mind numb, she absentmindedly began to check her voice mail. One message caught her attention. It was from Charlie Kellerman.

"Sarah, I have been reviewing the Implementation Plan for the improvements we need to make in engineering, and I am struck by the overlap between what I think we need to do and what you may be doing. I know John told us each to do our own thing, but I wonder if we should talk."

Sarah sat up straight. She had been thinking the same thing. John may have really tied her hands when he told her to leave Charlie and others alone. The reasons had all sounded good at the time, and Sarah had been relieved she did not have to mess with everything. However, she was coming to the conclusion that "messing with everyone" was exactly what she *should* be doing.

Two hours later, Sarah, Charlie, and their teams sat down for a joint conference on changes at Treetop. Roosevelt, one of Sarah's team members, was putting up a long piece of newsprint across one whole wall of the conference room. It looked like a giant fishbone diagram.

"Charlie," began Sarah, "I am really glad you called me. Our team has been thinking about all the changes that have to happen around here, and it is very obvious we cannot go our separate ways. We are going to have to work together." Charlie and his team studied the chart.

"Engineering is a key player in most of these changes," Sarah pointed out. "You are the driver of changes in engineering operations and the target of change in many of these other areas. Every one of these changes is critical to our ultimate goal. It's important that we integrate them, *especially* if we want to be able to seize opportunities that come our way in the delta stage. We need to be able to

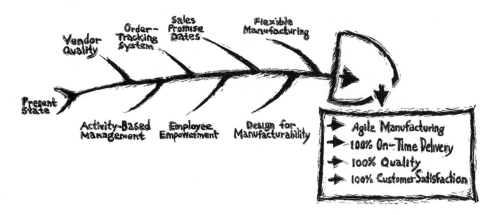

Figure 5.3
Fishbone Diagram of Change at Treetop

hear and respond to changes in the changes. I think we better check our change projects to be sure they are aligned and compare implementation plans. It is very likely we will find conflicting resource requirements and overlapping time frames."

"I agree," Charlie said. "And Sam from our team has been a strong advocate of making sure we have the kind of sponsorship we need for our changes. He'll show you the chart we put together analyzing the levels of sponsorship throughout the company."

Sam put up Charlie's organization chart full of circles, question marks, and asterisks.

"This is a real help," said Sarah. "We need to do this with each one of these changes. It's possible that someone who is a good sponsor for one change could be very bad for another. It also reinforces something I've been thinking about a lot. You have too, Charlie. Neither one of us can succeed at the changes John expects us to make without involving the management of every area of the company. John told me not to worry about engineering because you would take care of it, but it is clear today that we have to work together or we *will* be working in conflict.

"He also told me to leave Jack Cumberland in R&D alone until he got his feet wet, but we need him now. If he doesn't sign off on the change issues identified for each of the initiatives affecting his department, we can't very well expect him to be a good sponsor later.

"I know we are both worried about Keith Bailer's ability to deliver change in manufacturing," Sarah continued. "We need to collaborate with him, too. I am especially worried about Joe Schneider at South Bend. John specifically told me to let him alone. Joe has always been one of John's favorite people. He knows how hard it would be for Joe to change and said to work around him. He will be retiring soon, and then we can put someone in the job who is a good sponsor of change. Can we work around a plant manager and expect changes to happen in his plant? Do we have time to wait for Joe to retire?"

Charlie and his team nodded in agreement. "We've had these same conversations," Sam said. "We have been talking about going back to John to talk about sponsorship and what we need."

"Count our team in on that meeting," Sarah exclaimed.

"Charlie," Sarah continued, "I've been looking at the organization chart Sam just laid out for us. I wonder if there is something we should add to it. You had John identified as a good sponsor, but I see you changed him to questionable. I think you are right. He may need some help figuring out what being a good sponsor means, but he is very willing to do what it takes. Also, there is something else about this chart. John is the only one who is not changing. Is it possible to make changes in all these other areas and not expect that John will have to change as well? Look at our chart, the fishbone diagram. Does the president of a company act differently when he is president of a company delivering 100 percent on time with 100 percent quality and 100 percent customer satisfaction?"

Sarah began to make a list on the white board.

"What kind of president heads an organization that:

- Uses activity-based management to analyze cost and quality across department boundaries?
- Has strong supplier partnerships?
- Uses sophisticated relational databases on client servers to manage information?
- Has pushed decision-making responsibility and the authority required to do good work down to the shop floor and clerical level?
- Involves sales and *all* other departments in common goals, accountabilities, and rewards?

- Involves multiple areas of the company in product design?
- Has a manufacturing floor that can dissolve and reform in the blink of an eye?
- Manages an organization that is in constant flux and change?

"Maybe we should put a star next to John's name. He is going to have to change as well as sponsor change. What a big job we have!"

The two teams looked at the charts on the wall and then at each other with a mixture of excitement and fear in their eyes.

III. TOOLS FOR CHANGE

MEASURE THE SPONSORS

Once the criteria for being an effective sponsor is defined, the next step is to find the sponsors for your change and assess their current level of sponsorship. Then you will know how much change has to be made in the sponsorship before proceeding with the change. If you do not develop strong sponsorship, you must think seriously about whether or not to proceed with this change. Strong sponsorship makes change happen. Weak sponsorship kills change. It may be a long slow death, but often those are the worst kind!

Draw your organization chart. Identify the most senior person in the company with the authority and responsibility to support the change. Remember, because all the changes going on in the company have to fit into the company vision, the ultimate sponsor for even very specific changes is usually the most senior person in the organization.

Build a map of the sponsorship down through the organization to the lowest level of change required. Be sure to consider the ramifications of any change on other departments or business units in the company. Besides engineering, what other departments or areas will have to change to accomplish the engineering department changes?

After the map is finished, start at the very top and begin to assess each sponsor using the criteria discussed in this chapter. Where there is strong sponsorship, allow yourself a moment of rejoicing. Then plan how you will sustain that sponsorship and deal with it if it begins to slip. Also develop a contingency plan in case that particular sponsor disappears in the next reorganization.

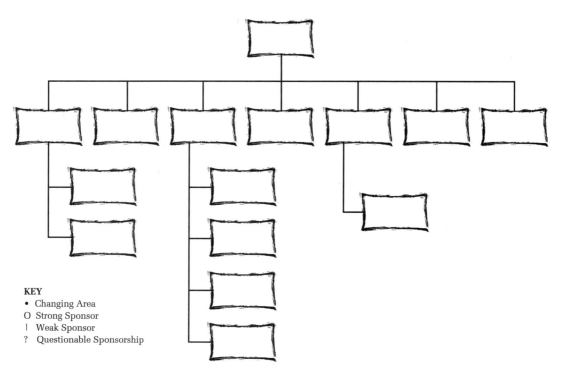

KEY
- Changing Area
- O Strong Sponsor
- | Weak Sponsor
- ? Questionable Sponsorship

Figure 5.4
Your Organization Chart and Sponsorship Strengths

Where the sponsorship is weak, build a plan of action. What do you need to do to increase the level of sponsorship? Is it a matter of education, training, or information sharing? Is the sponsor willing to learn? If not, what forces can be brought to bear on that sponsor to make the current state, the state of not sponsoring change, no longer acceptable? What will drive the sponsor into the delta to become a better sponsor?

6
Change Agents

Think of it as a high-risk assignment. Change agents must ask people to leave the comfort of what they know and put them in a place where the rules keep changing. This is not an easy task. However, the ability to help an organization survive in the delta, to move forward toward that ever-elusive future, is clearly a vital, important skill.

Those people who are serious about their careers and about making their companies successful had better develop these skills.

WHO ARE THE CHANGE AGENTS?

Change agents are the people who plan and support change. They are the project leaders, implementation team, first-line supervisor, union steward, clerk in accounts payable, and forklift truck driver on the third shift. Anyone and everyone who takes responsibility for figuring out how to make the changes happen and how to support the targets are the change agents.

Change agents who have managerial responsibility or authority to initiate change in their areas are also sponsors of change. Change agents are almost always targets as well. As a result of the changes they implement, they too will have to change.

Chipcom Corporation, located just outside of Boston, is serious about change. An incredible company with a strong, steady growth rate, it provides sophisticated networking capabilities to enhance its customers' ability to share information across

91

their companies. Chipcom recognizes that it must be in a permanent delta condition, allowing changes to take root and seed the next change. To be effective at creating that kind of environment, Chipcom has two super change agents, *Ken Kerber* and *Tony Venturoso*. Ken is responsible for training and development, working out of the human resource department. Tony is the director of Total Quality. Together they make a strong change management team. They are not responsible for every change in the company. They are responsible for helping the project change agents build a successful change strategy. Ken and Tony, working alongside those change agents, develop the sponsor skills of the senior management, design change communication systems and new reward systems, and build timely, appropriate education and training.

Their biggest job is to develop skilled change agents and sponsors throughout the whole company. They also help every employee, from the president to the shipping clerk, develop a high tolerance for change. Thanks to Ken, Tony, and the people they have helped to develop, everyone at Chipcom can live more comfortably in the delta with all its ambiguity and flux. They are helping place Chipcom in a strong competitive position for the future.

THE SUCCESSFUL CHANGE AGENT

If you understand the change process in Section 1 and the roles and responsibilities of the sponsor in Chapter 5, you have a good foundation for defining effective change agents.

Key Responsibility	Targeted Performance
Understand the Change	• Identify and measure the impact of the change on the people, structures, processes, and culture of the company. • Determine the level and type of sponsorship required. • Find the appropriate sponsors and transfer ownership of the change to the right sponsors. • Figure out the primary and secondary sources of resistance by target population.

Manage the Change	• Systematically apply the principles of effective change management:
	    1. Communication
	    2. Learning
	    3. Reward and reinforcements

	• Integrate multiple changes into a common plan and apply sound project-management principles to all the changes required.
Deal with People	• Listen and listen and listen and listen. • Translate the messages to targets and sponsors in language that is meaningful to them. • Build team strength at the project level, in the senior management group, and among target groups. • Develop effective coaching and counseling techniques. • Build organization and structure into the delta wherever and whenever possible. • Use some process, such as fishbone diagramming, to keep the changes in the delta identified, monitored, and tracked. • Use that process to keep the organization focused on changes in the delta while maintaining regular company business. • Know when to solve problems and how to do it effectively. • Know when to delegate and how to manage the delegated.

*J*ohn Benton, general manager of the *J. L. Clark division* of Clarco, is a good change agent. As general manager, John also sponsors change well—he rolls up his sleeves and gets right into the trenches to help make change happen. He doesn't just sit at his desk and order others to move into the delta.

When John decided that his operation had all kinds of bright and talented people who could contribute a lot more if the processes wouldn't get in their way, he wondered how to unleash all that talent and creativity. People had been kept under tight control for so long they had forgotten how to think in unorthodox ways and make unusual combinations of elements, how to add one plus one to make three. John figured he needed to understand what he was asking of his targets, so he began to explore how people become creative. He found a course at the local college in creative thinking, and he signed up. He even went a step further: he enrolled his eighteen-year-old daughter as well. He figured he could learn a lot more from the course if he learned from Dana's perspective. Of course, he was right. The course unleashed fabulous creativity in Dana (a lot more than it did in John). By watching her learn and learning from her as well as from the teacher, John accomplished two things: he improved his own creativity and he learned how others become more creative. Today, that learning continues within J. L. Clark.

CHARLIE

"You know, when this project is over I don't ever want to see a pizza again," laughed Tom.

"By the time this project is over, you'll be so old your teeth will all have fallen out and you won't be able to chew pizza," countered Sam.

The Engineering Improvement Task Force was polishing off the last of a 10-P.M. dinner, gathered around the conference table where they seemed to spend a lot of their time these days. They all sat silent for a few minutes, each of them staring at the big newsprint chart that covered the entire north wall of the room. The fishbone diagram they built in Sarah's office over two months ago covered the wall from floor to ceiling. It had undergone about six revisions in the past few months, defining the identified change elements and adding two new ones that neither team had originally recognized.

Time frames were added to most of the projects and numbers indicated projects that were in sequence, one dependent upon another, or on hold until resources were freed up from the first in the series. The Engineering Improvement Task Force had given a new name to their project, "Engineering Partnerships," and Sarah's group had given a new name to the future, "The 100 Percent Solution." The fishbone, with all the changes, had been unfurled for everyone in the company to see, and John Shane had explained how all these changes fit under The 100 Percent Solution. There were hoots of laughter and lots of scornful comments after the department meetings were over and John left. But Sarah's team had formed a separate task force made up of members from each change team. They did an excellent job of rolling out a series of communication efforts.

That first meeting with John was followed by a lot of intense communication between supervisors and their people. The supervisors had been carefully prepared and informed. They were given a lot of additional supporting data to explain things to people in more detail and to show them what was and was not known.

Things were coming along pretty well. That special communication task force came out of Sarah's efforts to unite all the changes. She invited each change's primary change agent to sit on a special 100 Percent Solution committee where all the changes could be monitored and integrated under the umbrella of the company's future. Charlie was the Engineering Partnership representative, and he was very excited about their progress.

The future was defined and the way things were in the present was pretty well identified. The changes that needed to be made were on paper. Next, the team had settled down to the most difficult job of all: planning the change. None of the team members had been relieved of their day-to-day responsibilities in order to deliver this change to engineering, so most of the work on the changes got done between 6 and 8 in the morning and after 4:30 at night. Pizza didn't necessarily help digestion or build good change agents, but the pizza place was the only fast-food restaurant in town that took pity on their busy schedule and delivered their food right to the office door.

Ever since Charlie had begun to understand the magnitude of the changes they were about to make, he had been worrying about the team's ability to make all this change happen. He'd asked for a meeting with Sally Jimnitz, the vice president of human resources, and told her of his concerns.

"You're right to raise this issue, Charlie. From what I know of your team, you've got some great people, but there is a lot we know about being a change agent that could help them. I've been giving this a lot of thought because we have so many ongoing projects and the change agents aren't all going to be equal in their abilities. So I've been doing some reading, and I just came back from a 'Managing Change as a Key Business Strategy' seminar at the Association for Manufacturing Excellence. I think I can help."

The Engineering Partnership Team, under Sally's guidance, sat down one morning several weeks later and outlined their job description as change agents. They then did an informal but very straightforward assessment of their own abilities and those of everyone else who would have to be a change agent. Sally then scheduled a workshop for the team and all the other change agents on effective change management strategies. They learned a lot.

Sam was proving to be an excellent change agent. He seemed to have natural insights, skills, and abilities that fit that job description. Tom was good, too, though he had a limited tolerance for resistance and agreed with the team that they needed to help him be more patient with targets who were having trouble with the changes. Jane seemed to be the least able to relate to those change issues that were not logical and measurable—that were not, as she said, "things you can get some numbers around." So she and the team had agreed that she would be responsible for the operational and structural parts of the planning and implementation, while Tom and Sam worried more about the people parts of the change. In the meantime, their weekly formal briefing sessions ensured that Jane kept up to speed on the people problems as well.

Charlie was pretty quiet as the pizza got cleared away and the group said its good-nights. On the surface, Charlie seemed to be doing great. He understood the things that Sally and the change-management consultant had taught him and his team. He came out well in the assessments they had done on themselves and each other. He seemed to be a good change agent, and he was. He knew what to do. Charlie was having a real inner battle, though, because he wasn't a very good target! As things moved along and the future was becoming more clear, Charlie could see that the role of the vice president of engineering would change a lot. Charlie had always been an excellent manager. He treated people with respect and worked hard to involve them. So he was racked by confusion the past few weeks over his discomfort with the changes. Weren't these changes going to result in a department that fit his management style? Weren't they in many ways formalizing things he had preached for years? What was wrong with him?

Susan, Charlie's wife, noticed his increasing distraction. She asked him about it several times, but he couldn't explain it to her. It didn't even make sense to him, but Susan was a very wise woman. Last Saturday night she announced the baby sitter was arriving at 7:00 and they were going out to dinner. Charlie was tired, but he shaved and got dressed and out they went. He was very glad they did. Over a quiet dinner in their favorite restaurant Susan helped him ferret out what was wrong.

"I want these changes for my people," Charlie explained. "But I kind of feel like there isn't going to be a place for me anymore. I really like Treetop. I don't like the idea of leaving, but I can't see myself there in another year or so."

"I don't understand," said Susan. "By next year at this time you will have the department you always talked about, the department you've been trying to create all your life. You know how to manage people who are independent and strong, and you so firmly believe in building bridges with the other departments. I've heard you say that countless times. Why wouldn't there be a place for you? I don't hear the future eliminating all management. Won't there still be a need for a vice president of engineering?"

"Yes," said Charlie, "Treetop is such an engineering-driven company we'll probably always need an engineering head, whether they call it vice president or not, but I don't think it will be me. I'm the guy who wanted these changes. I give a lot of energy to trying to convince others that it should happen. I liked being the lone voice crying out for change. I liked the image I had of myself as the only person who was right." Charlie stopped and looked at Susan in amazement. "That's it, Susan! That's the problem. I've always felt superior to the rest of the senior management because they were so stupid they couldn't see the need for these changes, much less what they could look like. Now we're all equals. It won't be as much fun anymore. Fighting for this management style was a lot more fun than managing this way. In fact, I don't think I really like managing this way. It's too easy!"

Charlie looked glumly into his wine. "I like the fight to change and the changing. I don't think I'm going to like the change." Susan was quiet, too, sitting and thinking about what Charlie had said. Then she roused herself.

"OK, Charlie. What you're saying makes a lot of sense to me. You like to change others, but you yourself never liked to change. Heck, you won't even change cars when they're on their last legs. So you're good at what you're good at. You're a great crusader and an excellent change agent, but a year from now you will have to change. So you are going to have to look at your options. Either you choose to change to a manager who is managing a department in which he believes, but no longer has to fight for, or you find some other part of Treetop that needs your current strengths, that change agent ability, or you will leave Treetop and find another company that needs and values your change-agent skills. None of those choices is bad, Charlie. You, and your family, can live with any choice you make. The good thing is you don't have to choose tonight. At least you understand what's been eating you. Now you can think about it and decide down the road. Right now, I want the biggest, gooiest, most evil dessert on the menu *and* another glass of that great wine! How about you?"

SARAH

A subtle change was taking place around Sarah. Along with all the overt, planned changes, she was beginning to notice another change, and she liked it. All through the early part of the year, as the changes were being identified and planned for, Sarah had felt a lot of pressure from people in the company who saw her as the cause of all this change. Before the big communication effort began, she had gotten a lot of negative push-back from people afraid of the changes. They had started to hold her responsible, to see her as the cause of the pain they anticipated. Sarah knew that wasn't good for the change project, and she didn't like it personally.

Now that was changing. There were clearly elements of the changes, both the future and the delta, that people didn't like. But they were giving her a lot of credit for doing a good job. They were beginning to recognize that her team and the other change teams knew what they were doing, and the employees now seemed to be willing to give them the benefit of the doubt. What a great feeling!

At least it had been a great feeling until about ten minutes ago. The change-management consultant Sally had brought in to help them figure out how to work with change had stopped by her office.

"Sarah," the consultant started, "could we talk about John Shane for a few minutes? I'm curious about something he said to me today at lunch, and I'd like to get your reactions. John is very pleased with the way things are going. He recognizes the work you and all the teams have done to make sure these changes happen with a minimum of pain. Ted Lamm told him the Framingham people were very impressed with the implementation plan you gave him. In fact, they said that if Treetop could pull off these changes successfully, there is a lot more business that could be put on the table. The momentum is building nicely, too. It looks like a lot of change is going to happen very fast, but people seem to be ready for it. What bothers me is what he said next: 'Sarah's changes are going to make this company really strong. I can't wait to see what she delivers!'" The consultant sat quietly for a moment as Sarah thought about what she had just heard.

At first, she felt nothing but great pride. It was great that John recognized her efforts and what her people were doing. He was right. Things were going well, but as she sat in silence and mulled over his words a bell went off in her head. "Sarah's changes!!!!! These aren't *my* changes," she exclaimed. "They belong to the people in the departments, change agents, targets, and sponsors. I'm just laying out a path and a process for getting there. I don't own the changes. These are John's changes. He saw the need for them. He's sponsoring them. It's not a good idea for people to see them as my changes. It makes them lazy. They'll look to me not only to deliver the change process, but to deliver the changes. I can't do that. They have to do that. This is *not* my change!"

"You're right, Sarah, but this isn't the first time I've heard this. It's great that everyone sees what you are doing in terms of laying out the process for changing. It gives them confidence to see you and to know that you know what you are doing. It's going to help a lot, but if they see the changes themselves as being 'Sarah's changes,' they won't take the ownership they need, especially the people in the sponsor cascade."

Sarah sighed. "I guess there *is* one change I have to make myself. I have to transfer ownership of these changes to the people in this company. I'm a good change agent. I can figure out how to make that happen."

After the consultant left, Sarah turned her attention to the other task on her desk for the day. She was proud of the skills her change agents were building for themselves, but she had held a gripe session with all the change teams two days ago, a chance to vent and blow off some steam and check what things were getting in their way and what resources they needed. There had been an explosion of complaints from almost every change agent in the room over one issue: performance measurement. Other than Sarah and a couple of her immediate team members, no change agent was dedicated to the change project 100 percent of the time. All of them had regular duties as well. They were doing an incredible job of finding odd hours and extra hours to do this work, but as the load increased, their managers were beginning to pressure them about their regular work.

"I know I'm not being as attentive to my regular job," many of them said. "Next fall, when my manager sits down to do my performance review, how much credit am I going to get for all this extra time? Will I get criticized for the fact that my regular work slipped? Is my manager adding this effort to my job responsibilities? I could do a great job as a change agent and find no raise or bonus, or even a negative rating at the end of the year. Can you do something about this, Sarah?"

Suddenly Sarah was struck by an interesting paradox. The conversation she just had with the consultant and the gripe session of two days ago tied together. Of course, the management had not altered their performance criteria for the change agents. Part of that was Sarah's fault. She needed to teach the management group that supporting the change agents was an important part of their change sponsorship. But she also realized that the managers *still* did not own these changes and their role in them. She was sure she could help them learn, but it was also common sense. Why weren't they doing it? Because they saw them as Sarah's changes—not theirs. Now she had a clue for where to start transferring ownership for the changes.

III. TOOLS FOR CHANGE

BUILD THE CHANGE AGENTS
Step 1.

Identify the change agents in your change project. Map them as either change agents within the regular organizational structure of the company or as special change agents assigned to the project in a staff capacity. Note that some of them will have both responsibilities.

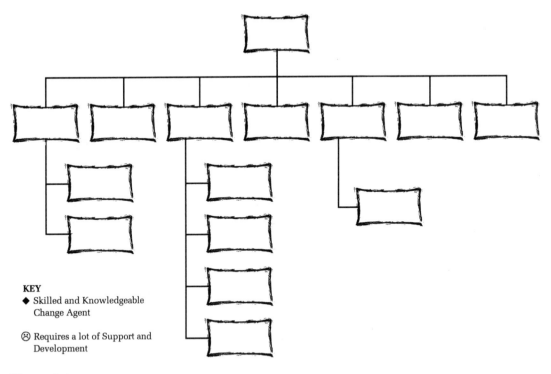

KEY

◆ Skilled and Knowledgeable
   Change Agent

☹ Requires a lot of Support and
   Development

Figure 6.1
Organizational Chart of Change Agents

Step 2.

Assess the skills and knowledge of each of the change agents and design a
plan to strengthen, work around, or replace them.

_____

_____

_____

_____

_____

_____

_____

_____

_____

Step 3.

Build a performance-measurement criteria for effective change agents and have it inserted into the performance management system so they can be evaluated fairly in the delta.

_____

_____

_____

_____

_____

_____

_____

_____

7
The Targets of Change

I. ELEMENT OF CHANGE

Some people welcome change; others flee from it. Even those who welcome change do *not* want to change certain parts of their lives: a favorite pen, for instance, or their word-processing software. Even people with very high tolerance for change can only handle so much before they cry "Enough!"

Why do people have such a range of tolerance? Why are some changes easier to make than others? Culture, religion, upbringing, genes, and chemistry all play a part in the rich variety of change tolerance. There is no easy formula for predicting a general population's (or an individual's) tolerance for change.

Yet change agents are responsible for helping targets move through the delta and cope with change. People within companies will survive only if they increase their tolerance and learn to live with constant change and a fluid work environment. That does not mean that people will not resist changes. Resistance is not a bad thing. Opposition to a change forces sponsors and change agents to examine the future and the change process. Well-managed opposition keeps a healthy tension between the old and the new and helps everyone monitor and improve change.

How can resistance be managed? Companies need to understand the sources of resistance. They need to help targets understand and express their resistance in safe, easy ways. Then they can work in partnership with the targets to:

- Reduce the resistance
- Change the change, or
- Help the targets to cope with their resistance.

That is change management.

As you examined the stages of the change process—the future, present, and delta—you have already seen the sources of resistance to change.

THE FUTURE
A Clear Definition

When targets can look at the future and see it clearly, they compare that future to the present. If they see it as undesirable, they resist. Sponsors and change agents who want to reengineer their organizations see the tremendous possibilities in a future that throws away conventional thinking and challenges current processes, enabling their organization to develop a totally new paradigm. Targets, frequently the department head or other middle managers, often fear that future state. They cannot see a problem that needs fixing, nor a need to move to that future state. They can't see why, if things need to be improved, they should not just do a better job at what they currently do. After all, this way worked well for over twenty years. Can't they just put their heads together and make it better? Why do they have to throw it away when it has worked so well?

Peter M. Senge, in *The Fifth Discipline,* writes of this reluctance to change.

> *Whenever there is "resistance to change," you can count on there being one or more "hidden" balancing processes. Resistance to change is neither capricious nor mysterious. It almost always arises from threats to traditional norms and ways of doing things. Often these norms are woven into the fabric of established power relationships. The norm is entrenched because the distribution of authority and control is entrenched. Rather than pushing harder to overcome resistance to change, artful leaders discern the source of the resistance. They focus directly on the implicit norms and power relationships within which the norms are embedded.*

Often targets see the future state as threatening. New technology will mean eliminating 20 percent of the people in the finance department. The new organizational structure calls for skills and knowledge the targets don't have and can't imagine they will be able to develop. The new process makes their life harder; they will have to work ten-hour shifts instead of eight hours a day. They will have to move their work location to a different part of the office with fewer windows and less space. They will have to work with the people in inventory control, and everyone knows how unfriendly those people are.

The police department of a major city invested serious dollars in a special tracking system installed in the police cars. Designed to send a constant signal back to headquarters, it was considered a major safety device by police management. It was considered a major intrusion by the police officers who saw it as a "Big Brother" tactic on the part of management. Obviously, management did not trust them and was using this device to spy on them. What did management think they would find out, that police were spending too much time getting doughnuts or stopping at their girlfriend's or boyfriend's house or picking up their laundry? The police officers' mistrust of this "future state" resulted in serious resistance. The devices seemed to "break" with great regularity. They fell out of cars, got run over, and became victims of other creative damage. The cost of repair and replacement became prohibitive.

Several weeks into the program, two policemen found themselves surrounded by a group of angry "bad guys." They radioed for backup, but the crowd moved in on them before they could give their location. The dispatcher sent backup units to the blinking light on his screen and the officers were rescued. Word spread that the honing device had saved two officers' lives. But the city council, having heard too many stories for too long about high repair costs, pulled the plug on the program. The homing device could have saved more lives in the future, but the change was not tolerated because it was seen as "bad" by the targets.

Chapter 3 discussed how strong the drive is to stay in the present state. The comfort and security of the present are especially strong when the future is unknown. If the future state is fuzzy or ill defined, or it is difficult for the target to picture his or her role there, it is very difficult to sign up to go there.

The future state will never be static or perfect. Those who look at it and see that some current problems and issues will still be there are also reluctant to change: "Well, they certainly have a better solution to the problem of poor-quality raw materials, but it is obvious to me that they don't have a clue about how to deal with the log jam created by the flow of raw materials into the plant. They have only solved half the problem. They need to figure them all out before they expect me to change."

Yet the very nature of effective change means leaving out details of the future state as change begins. The company sets the outside boundaries, determines what is firm, and begins the change process. For many, this sparks incredibly difficult questions. "What will it look like?" "What will be expected of me?" "What won't change?" "What will stay the same?"

When these questions cannot be answered, a lot of people pull back. "I'll sign up when they have this thing better defined. Right now, they don't know what they're doing."

THE PRESENT

While the future repels, confuses, and frightens the targets, the present offers comfort and security. It is known. It requires little effort. It has strong built-in sources of satisfaction. If parts of the present don't make sense, don't work, or don't create success, they can be justified and explained away.

> **W**hen *O. J. Simpson* was arrested for the murder of his former wife, Nicole Brown-Simpson, the country was forced to take a long hard look at battered wives. The recurring question was why a woman would continue to have a relationship with a man who threatened and hurt her. In interview after interview the student of change can hear the rationalization for continuing the current state. Although the present is a place of danger, the women weigh that danger against what they perceive to be positive in the present. Based on that perception, many choose to stay until it is too late.

Companies run a serious risk when they do not analyze the reasons people would choose to stay in the present state or when they treat those reasons lightly. At the top of the organization, the senior management can clearly see that the present state is killing the organization. Without change the company will die, the plant will close, the product line will dry up. Why can't all the people in the company see this? Why are they fighting the changes? Don't they see that they are only hurting themselves?

Some do see this and yet they choose not to change. They *would* rather die than change. Some do not see that the present is bad—at least for them. Yes, the plant might close and the production move to another location, but it would take at least two years. In two years, they can retire or have enough invested to start that little business they have been dreaming about for years.

Some can't see the dangers in the present state the way that the senior management does. It just doesn't make sense to them. How can this be happening? Those numbers must be wrong. Some people don't think in numbers; the numbers don't make any sense to them. They think in terms of how much work-in-progress is on the floor, and there's plenty of it right now.

Some understand the numbers, but they don't believe them. Management has been threatening for years that the competition would get ahead of them, and it hasn't yet. Management tried to scare them three years ago with some numbers that showed the decreasing profitability, but the company is still here, isn't it? Management made them install that new manufacturing system and spent two million dollars on it. It didn't change a thing, and this operation still runs just like it always did. They are just out two million dollars.

Sometimes targets are just tired.

> The company has been around for 52 years. During all that time, union and management fought, and the workers were caught in the middle. Business has swung up, then down. The company centralized, then decentralized. When it made money, it moaned that it didn't make enough. When it had a loss, it moaned that it didn't make enough. The workforce has lived with tension and fear for the past five years as it has seen work-in-process reduced, profits go down, and market share go to its competitors. Over those years they have tried a variety of tactics to stem the hemorrhaging. Now everyone is tired. Sitting in a workshop on change management at the start of a major reengineering effort, one of the targets, a first-line supervisor, said softly with a tremor in his voice, "Sometimes I wish they would stop trying. Why don't they just say enough and pull the plug? Let's shut it down and board it up. You have to know when to quit."

Management Style

When people resist leaving the present state, the company has to ask itself if it did anything to create that resistance. Past messages may have taught people to value the present and feel a sense of betrayal if they changed. The military model that formed the basic company design created a culture of entitlement. "Come and work here, and in exchange for your labor we will give you money, benefits, and security. We, the management, will make the decisions. You, the worker, will do what you are told. As a result, we will get paid a lot more than you." Workers may not have liked the contract, but it was the only game in town. So they signed on.

Now the system is changing, and logic says workers should like the new future. They will be partners in the company, contributing their ideas and working *with* management to make things consistently better. After all, these are people capable of managing their own personal lives, raising children, running the Boy Scouts, paying off mortgages, and building boats in their garages. Clearly, they can make a greater contribution to company operations if we could only harness all that ability, but the contract companies operated under for so long has left its mark. People learned to "park their brains at the door." After a while they learned to live with that. They are not sure they want to change.

Change Orientation

Over time employees learned to judge the values of the company from its behaviors. One important value for companies today is the ability to change rapidly with minimum pain. Companies need to know what they have taught the organization in the past about change. How did they handle the change process in the past? Did they care that there was pain and strive to reduce it? Were they successful in achieving change? Past records are often poor, as those 400 engineers in Dallas pointed out. It seems that many organizations have demonstrated to employees that they do not know how to change. They do not value change.

Successful change and a process for making change happen do not appear to be built into organizational cultures. Companies have some work to do; the culture must integrate the value of change, change management, and change supportive behaviors into the organization. If not, employees will resist change—even those they feel are good—because they do not believe those changes can happen.

THE DELTA

Even when the future state is desirable and the present state clearly is not, it is hard to change. The delta is vast, long, and threatening. Targets have many foreboding questions about the delta.

- How will we get from here to there?
- How will we manage all this extra work?
- Will we have to change all at once or in stages?
- What can I take with me from the present? What do I have to leave behind?
- Will the company go too fast? Too slow?
- Will I have a chance to say good-bye to what I leave behind?
- Do we have enough money to make this change?
- What will we do if things start to slip as we go through the delta?
- What if they've made the wrong choice for the future; can we go back?

EXPRESSING RESISTANCE

If you are very lucky (or very smart), you will know when people are resisting the changes you propose. They will tell you. They will tell you in words and actions if you give them both the opportunity and a framework for their resistance.

That framework is very important. Senior management often expresses willingness to hear about the resistance people feel. So they hold "Breakfast with the President" meetings or travel to all their locations for large meetings. There, after giving a speech complete with slides full of numbers and graphs, they stand at the podium, brace their arms firmly and ask, "Are there any questions?

We want to know what you are thinking. Please, this is your chance to ask." Then 200 or 500 or 50 people sit silently and avoid the president's eyes.

Make it easy for targets to express their fears and concerns. Make it safe for them to do so. Not safe by your criteria, but by theirs. If they perceive that asking a question in a large meeting is not safe, it *is not* safe for them. If they don't want to be seen by their co-workers signing up for "Breakfast with the President" because they will be perceived as selling out, that is their truth. So smart companies find a rich variety of ways to allow people to seek information and express their concerns.

People frequently cannot articulate their concerns. They need help to formulate their questions and express their fears and anxieties. Company changes are often broad and deep and have broad and deep ramifications. Many people feel in their hearts that these changes are wrong or bad, but they cannot always explain their reasons for feeling that way. They are operating from a gut-level reaction that may be very hard for them to articulate.

Many reasons people do not want to change are very personal. The engineering draftsman has watched those young kids coming into the department for several years now. They are comfortable and deft in their operation of the CAD system from the day they walk in. They scare him. They seem to know so much more about engineering than he does. Now he too is expected to become comfortable and fluent on the CAD system. He is concerned about his ability to learn to use the software. That much he understands, but there is something more. It is something he can't easily express because he really does not understand it himself. That CAD system has become a symbol of the young, smart, and threatening.

Sure he can learn some software and a new way of drafting, but can he be like those kids? Probably not. Yet he now has to do what they do and use the tools they use. The thought of those tools makes him anxious. The engineer cannot always see this. He certainly can't put it into the form of a question to the president at the general meeting—"Excuse me, sir. I appreciate the need for us to use this technology to stay competitive and gain back the market share we are losing to competitors who can get new products to market faster, but what will you do about the nausea I feel every morning when I look at those hot-shot young engineers and figure I will never be as good as them, even if I learn to use the same tools they use. What are you going to do to make me feel better?"

Presidents don't hear those questions. People do not know how to ask them. Even when they do have the words, they usually do not choose to take that risk.

BUILDING A TOLERANCE FOR CHANGE

Because change is a constant, an ongoing element of every successful organization, it is critical that people learn to tolerate it. Tolerance does not mean eliminating all resistance to change, but it does mean creating organizations where
the natural resistance of individuals and groups is not considered an aberration
or enemy that must be fought down and defeated.

Rather, change processes must be well structured and consistent. This means
people can begin to trust that while any new change may engender fear, frus-
tration, and sadness, they can count on the company to value those feelings,
address them, and help the individual get through them.

As time goes on in this kind of environment, people develop a high tolerance
for change. They do not blindly accept each change because the company says
it is good, but they do trust the process of change and walk comfortably
between the extremes of resistance and acceptance.

Despite the very best efforts, some people will choose *not* to change. Some will
not be able to make the adjustment to a specific change. Others will never
become comfortable in a fluid, rapidly changing environment. When you have
done everything you can to help them build that tolerance and they cannot or
will not, you have to make a choice. Is there a place in the organization for
them? If so, what is the impact on the specific changes and the change-focused
environment you are building? If you can afford the impact, you may choose to
keep them.

If you cannot afford that impact, you need to help these people out of the organization. They should not go out in defeat! Being unwilling or unable to
change should not negate the years of contribution they have made to the organization. They need to see that you recognize and value their contribution. The
rest of the organization needs to see that as well. The company changes
because it must. Those who do not change with the company will not go into
the company's future, but they will not be dishonored or thrown away. They
will leave with the knowledge that you value their help in getting the company
this far.

It was his firm. He was the majority stockholder and the son of the founder. His
father's will, passing the company on to him, had been full of strong words about
always 'taking care of the legacy.' He could not do it. The company clearly needed
a management style he did not understand or know how to emulate. He had tried.
He went to seminars and workshops. He had an assessment of his leadership
style done by a blind group of people in the company, but it apparently had not
changed. The company had moved a long way to a highly participative style of

> management and had integrated a lot of functions to improve the way work got done, but he hadn't improved and he knew it.
>
> So he was resigning. It hurt. He hoped his father would have understood. He wasn't sure he understood himself, but he knew he had to get out of the way. He was surprised that he was not angry, but he was very, very sad.

The Tactics of Tolerance

The sources of resistance are also the sources of the tactics to reduce it. You can learn how to reduce resistance by systematically analyzing the reasons why people resist change. Then you can design a process for dealing with people and minimizing inevitable resistance at each stage in the change process.

There appear to be three keys to reducing resistance in each stage of the change process:

- Communication
- Learning
- Rewards and reinforcements

Part 3 will address those three change management mechanisms and how to build them.

II. REAL WORLD   *Treetop Manufacturing Company*

CHARLIE

"Charlie, you've gone crazy! This is getting out of hand. It wasn't so bad when you and that 'team' of yours began to play around with engineering, but now you're joining forces with that group of Sarah's. They're throwing everything up for grabs. This is nuts! We're going to destroy everything that was good around here, and you are a party to it. It has got to stop!"

Charlie sat quietly through Keith Bailer's tirade at the lunch table. Keith was the vice president of manufacturing. Months ago, when Charlie realized that he could not make changes in engineering without involving other departments, he and his team had drawn a map of the organization and determined where they had strong sponsorship for their changes. Keith was one he had listed as a good sponsor. Now he wasn't so sure. What was this all about? Keith had invited him out to lunch, and as soon as they had placed their orders he had jumped into this tirade. His face was red with the intensity of his message, and he had leaned close to Charlie, close enough that Charlie could feel his anger and pain.

"Keith, calm down," Charlie implored. "What's got you so riled up? What's your problem? You've been complaining for years that things weren't good around here. Now we've got a shot at fixing them and you're all worked up. What's the matter with you?"

"You're OK, Charlie. The changes you have laid out in your department make a lot of sense. I know you have got to get better systems and get your people to use them. I like the idea of involving my production people in the design stages. You're right. Those are the things I've been wanting to see for years, but this whole change business is getting out of control. Sarah has gone off the deep end! She's eliminating the whole quality function. Hell, incoming raw materials have so many problems I have to put double inspections on them. We can't eliminate those guys. She wants my people practically married to the sales department. That won't work! Those guys need some controls over them. Sarah's always talking about partnerships among departments. Who is she kidding? Nobody can partner with sales. Those prima donnas will run rough shod over my people. I can work with you guys, Charlie, but not with them. That's crazy! I heard yesterday that she's going to eliminate the finance department. That woman is dangerous, Charlie. What's next after finance goes? Manufacturing?"

Charlie listened carefully to Keith, to his words and to his tone. He had learned a lot over the past few weeks about change. Some of that learning had come from his own issues. He was beginning to understand what it meant to be a target of change, how hard it was to know where those feelings came from and what they meant.

Now, he knew he had a problem sitting across from him at the lunch table. He had counted on Keith to be a good sponsor. There were a lot of changes that were going to occur in manufacturing, but Keith wasn't ready to sponsor these changes. Right now Keith was acting like a target of change, a target who was not too happy with the changes on the table. Keith would not be a good sponsor of these changes unless he dealt with his own feelings as a target.

That's exactly what he was doing. He *was* dealing with those feelings by dumping them on Charlie's plate and getting Charlie to help make them go away. Charlie was getting better at listening, though. He heard Keith's concerns as concerns about how these changes were bad for the company, but what about Keith himself? How did he feel personally about these changes? Charlie began to probe behind Keith's words.

Charlie and Keith sat at the lunch table in earnest conversation for almost two hours. What came out of Charlie's insistent, thoughtful questioning was a lot of change issues. Keith admitted that Joan Schwartz, the plant manager at Lexington, seemed a lot better than Keith at understanding the changes the 100 Percent Solution team was proposing. Joan was ambitious and was always on Keith's tail. Was Keith's job in jeopardy?

Keith was also worried about Joe Schneider. Joe had been his mentor many years ago. Keith knew Joe would never be able to adjust to these changes, and he wasn't ready to retire. Was he going to have to fire Joe?

There was another major issue burning Keith. "Charlie, what if you guys are wrong? What if you are making the wrong changes? Where is it guaranteed that this is the way we should do things?"

Charlie thought of Ken Willinger in his own department. Ken had asked that same question over three months ago, but Charlie had never really answered it. Ken never asked again. In fact, Ken didn't say much of anything.

"This change business is hard," thought Charlie as he watched Keith gulp down his fourth cup of coffee. "We sat in our little team room and dreamed up these great changes all by ourselves. We thought we were pretty great change agents to initiate a partnership with Sarah and her team. But look at all these other partners we have ignored. I guess we thought they would just sit quietly and wait for us to get everything right. Then we expected them to just accept it because we had done such a great job of designing the future."

Charlie paid for lunch that day. He figured Keith had already done him a big favor. He had taught him a good lesson about change management. Charlie headed back to his office to put that lesson into practice.

SARAH

The 100 Percent Solution team did a survey. With the help of Sandra Jimnitz and the human resources department they designed a survey and sent one to each of the company's 1,100 employees. The team was confident that their work up to this point had given them a good picture of the present state. In anticipation of announcing the future state, they decided they wanted to know just *how* dissatisfied people were with the way things were today.

They knew customers were dissatisfied. They had done a good job of sampling them and their concerns in their preliminary work. Now they wanted to know how people inside the organization perceived problems. The survey results were fascinating. No one was happy with the current state! The same problems that the team had identified kept coming up over and over again. Quality and communication were the two greatest problems mentioned. There were two questions on the survey that really intrigued the team:

• The majority of our problems would be resolved if only other departments would straighten themselves out.	True	False
• When we are unable to do our best it is almost always an internal problem in our department.	True	False

Eighty-seven percent of the people from every department answered true to the first question. Almost the same number, over 83%, answered false to the second.

The team sat with Sarah in the 'War Room' trying to make sense of these results. "It appears that people see themselves as doing a good job, despite the problems created by others," observed Roosevelt. "That fits in with our results from the process analysis. People really try to do a good job, but the processes get in their way."

"These answers may be pointing us to a problem, though," said Sarah. "If they think the problem is someone else, not the process, they will be looking for us to fix that 'someone else.' They may not be willing to make the kind of dramatic changes in their area that the new processes will require. They've been coming to work every day for years trying hard to do what was right and what made sense to them. They saw others as getting in their way. They may be hoping we will just 'change' those other people. They may be in for a big surprise when they see how much they have to change."

The team sat and looked at the survey results. Like Charlie, they were beginning to realize how much more work there was to do in this change management process.

III. TOOLS FOR CHANGE

HELPING TARGETS UNDERSTAND THEIR RESISTANCE

When targets become partners in change they understand the change process as well as change agents and sponsors do. When they have vehicles for identifying and quantifying their unease or their fear they can put their feelings into a sensible context that they can begin to deal with. Effective change agents provide targets with education regarding change and the change process, and give targets ways to put their resistance into an understandable format.

One of the first steps is to analyze the changes from the target's perspective. This helps change agents design communication, learning, and reward systems.

The Present

What about the present makes the targets secure/safe?

_____

_____

What will be lost when targets leave here?

_____

_____

The Delta

What is threatening about the transition . . .

From the company perspective?

_____

_____

From a personal perspective?

_____

_____

The Future

What is threatening about the future . . .

From the company perspective?

_____

_____

From a personal perspective?

_____

_____

PROVIDING SAFE FORMS TO EXPRESS RESISTANCE

Once targets understand their issues, they need a variety of safe ways to express that resistance to sponsors and change agents.

One-on-one meetings, surveys, focus groups, gab sessions, and pizza and beer after hours are all good methods. Create your own opportunities for targets to communicate their concerns, questions, and fears.

Use a survey to give targets the opportunity to answer the following questions:

These are the things about this change that cause me concern.

	No Concern	Some Concern	Serious Concern
I can't see how this change will solve our problems.			
I'm not sure we even have a problem.			
I don't think we are solving the right problem.			
There is too much extra work involved in this change.			
Management above me is not committed to this change.			
It looks to me like I could lose my job as a result of this change.			
I don't understand what people expect from me in this change.			
I don't know whether I will be able to do the job after it is changed.			
We have never been able to make change like this happen before.			
My work area has managed to keep a lot of inefficiencies and poor performance hidden from management. These changes may bring those things out in the open. I may get in trouble.			
I don't like the people I will have to work with/for in the future.			

The Tools of Change: The Change Systems

Although many of the specific reasons why people will or will not change may seem illogical, the change process itself has a very logical basis. The present is never totally secure and stable. There are always pressures pushing against it: changes in the marketplace, customer demands, and competitor innovations. The present is in a constant tension between the need to remain stable and the need to spill out into the delta and change. The change agents tip the balance between the drive for stability and the drive toward change so that the organization and all its employees choose to give up the present and move into the delta. The change agents need to do a good job of framing the future, assessing the present state, and shifting the balance to move people into and through the delta. Three tools will help change agents as they help others through the process:

1. A Communication System
2. A Learning System
3. A Reward and Reinforcement System

Obviously, if people are going to move, they need to know that the present state is no longer as sturdy and supportive as it was in the past. They also need to know what the future looks like. To satisfy these needs you have to communicate with them.

However, this is where many companies make their most serious change management mistake. They think that communication is enough. A carefully constructed *communication system* is an important tool in the change process, but it is not enough.

If communication is effective, people have a clear understanding of why they need to change, where they are going, and how the company will help them through the delta.

Communication, however, does not guarantee they will choose to change. They may choose not to change because they do not know how to be successful in the future. They may lack skills, knowledge, and tools to operate successfully anywhere but where they are. Therefore, the change agents must provide a carefully designed and executable *learning system* to enable people to change. Building those skills, dealing with new behaviors, and creating an environment for constant growth is critical.

But that is still not enough. People who understand the need to change and have the skills to change may *still* choose not to change. Why? Because the balance has not been shifted. Because the rewards they value are still in the present. Therefore, change agents, in their initial planning process, must build a *reward system* that alters that balance. They must make the present state unrewarding, put the rewards in the future state, and develop a series of incremental rewards as part of the support structure to get people through the delta.

Like any good tool set, these three systems do not exist in isolation. This is an integrated set of resources for the change agent. Clearly communicating the future helps people understand what they can do and what they do not know how to do. This drives the design and implementation of a learning system. Education and training by themselves, however, do not cause changes in behavior. The reward system must be adjusted so that new skills, behaviors, and levels of competency are rewarded. Behaviors and skills valued today, but no longer valid in the future, do not receive the rewards they have in the past. This change in the reward system must be communicated.

And so the circle goes round and round. . . .

8
The Communication System

ADJUSTING THE BALANCE
Leaving the Present State

The present is no longer desirable. You know that. The company knows that. But to spill people out of the stability of the present, you need to tell them why the present is no longer desirable. Tell them everything they need to know so they can make the decision to change. Tell them what forces, inside and outside the company, are driving these changes. If those forces are already having an impact on the company, tell them where and how much. If the impact of those forces is not felt yet, but you can see it coming, show them the evidence you used for that conclusion.

Be very careful as you describe what is not working. Do not attribute blame to employees or management. What is not working now used to work. You need to change the very things that made the company successful up until now: the tools, communication processes, decision-making process, and organizational structure. Why is the company changing? Those "old" ways are not stupid, but they will no longer work. Roger Martin in an article for *The Harvard Business Review,* "Changing the Mind of the Corporation," encourages change agents to "find out the good reasons why they [management] have come to act the way they do." There was a reason companies did things the way they did, and for a long time they were successful doing things that way.

In Indiana, *Fasson Industries* has a plant that makes pressure-sensitive papers for the stationary business. On the third shift, every night about 2 A.M., you can go out into the Fasson plant and find a young man driving a forklift truck, loading product

121

into eighteen-wheelers parked in the loading bays. He works for a company that is changing. He knows why it is changing. You can ask him. He will tell you what the company's present state is, what their customers need from them, and the quality level of their products. He will tell you what their competitors are doing and what the industry problems are. He can explain that the company that solves those problems will be the winner! He knows Fasson's market share and cost and profitability figures. He will tell you if those numbers are better or worse than last year.

He is different from millions of people working first, second, and third shifts in many companies going through major change. They do *not* know why they are changing. They think that management has just cooked up these changes to annoy people, as an excuse to downsize, close the operation, get rid of the union, or make more money for themselves!

Fasson has a much better chance of succeeding than the companies for whom other people work. Fasson understands change, the change process, and how to use communication as a tool for change. Fasson's management know that the stability of the present state will result in Fasson's failure in the future. They must destabilize the present. That fork lift truck driver proves that Fasson is using effective communication techniques to make that happen.

Will people understand what you are trying to tell them? They will if you package your message using their perspective, language, and orientation. Talk in their language, use their analogies, and highlight what is important to them. It allows them to relate. Show them the cost of *not* changing by sharing news of decreased profitability even when sales are rising. If you are talking to the engineering department tell them in their language; use their analogies, their buzz words. Change your message when you talk to the customer service reps, the shop floor, and the sales people in the remote sites. It is no accident that the forklift driver at Fasson can tell you about the instabilities of the present. That information is shared with him on a regular basis in words, analogies, and stories that make sense to *him*.

Throughout the early part of the 1990s the *Clinton Administration* struggled to change the U.S. health care system. We struggled to understand what they were doing. A massive amount of information was shared. Charts, diagrams, lists, and page after page of discussion were presented in the news media and by the White House. Yet all of the Clinton efforts were severely threatened by one health insurance commercial showing two people, Harry and Louise, in a comfortable setting talking about the changes that would take place in their health insurance coverage if the plan went into effect. The commercial represented the Health Insurance Association of America's interpretation of the plan's results. The Clintons were furious. That simple commercial put the plan into a frame of reference that millions of people could understand. In sixty seconds it undid miles of words, charts, and diagrams. 286,000 people called the toll free number that followed the ad. Harry and Louise made a complex topic simple. Those who thought the commercial didn't sound quite right had no alternative as simple and clean for comparison.

Defining the Future

Show people where they are going. Show them what you know about the future, and tell them what you do not know. In most companies the employees are absolutely certain that senior management has minutely defined the future. They think management has an extraordinarily detailed future state plan, complete with the names of those who will and will not survive and the succession plan for the next fifteen years! They will tell you that the only copy of the plan is locked in the president's safe, behind the picture of his kids on the office wall. Whenever the senior management assembles in this office and closes the door, they get out the plan to look at it and add names to the "Did Not Survive The Change" list.

Employees think this because they do not see anything else. They cannot believe management does not know where it is taking the company. In the past, stability meant that management acted like a parent and always knew what was good for employees. Employees assume this is happening again. To believe otherwise would fly in the face of the current culture.

Employees think management has a secret plan because management has not shown them what it does know and what it does not know. Management has not shown employees the process it is using to define the future. Management has not invited employees to contribute to the process.

Kaiser Aluminum's Trentwood, Washington, rolling mill plant is defying that assumption. *Ray Milchovich,* the general manager, has assembled a group of over 100 change agents from the 1,600-employee operation. The change agents are made up of supervisors, union grievers, and hourly employees from each functional operation in the plant. Organized into "Planning Councils," they are charged to design the future of Trentwood. Ray and the union leadership form the "Works Council," whose job is to set the outside boundaries of the future for the whole operation. The books are open. Current information and future projections are shared with the workers, the union, and the entire management cascade. That openness, in and of itself, is a change at Trentwood, which operated in the past as a typical unionized manufacturing operation.

Is it working? It is hard. The Works Council and individual Planning Councils have to get past a lot of old values that said, "Don't trust the information that comes from senior management." Some people at Trentwood still believe Ray has a secret master plan locked in a safe in his office, but the number of those people is growing smaller. More and more union members out in the plant say, "No, that's not true!" in response to a co-worker's lunch-time assertion that there is still hidden information. That is effective communication. That is effective change management.

There are four elements of the communication system that address the future:

1. Communicate what is known about the future.
   - Use examples, stories, and descriptions not just general slogans like: "We Will Be the Best At Servicing the Customer."
   - Try adding:
     When a customer says they want their order delivered on the 14th of next month it will be delivered on the 14th—right to the designated docking bay, loaded into the truck in the order that works best for them, with absolutely no rejects. There will be no paperwork enclosed with the order. The entire order's bar code stickers will correspond to an EDI exchange that enters the order into our accounts receivable system and the customer's accounts payable system simultaneously.

     The customer will have a direct line of communication open with the engineers who modified the product for that special order, the workers on the shop floor who built it in a team environment, and the customer support people who stop by or call to ensure that the customer is satisfied.

2. Communicate what is not known about the future.
   - If you are not sure that you can continue to keep open plants with a cost level over 7 percent, say so.
   - If you cannot predict the impact of a competitor's shortened time to market, say so.
   - If you cannot currently determine your company's product mix three years from now, say so.
   - Show the undecided, unformed, and changing nature of the definition of the future. Let targets see that the future is a moving target, impacted by the change process itself.

3. Communicate the process you are using to define the future.
   - Show employees the data you are using and their sources.
   - Describe the process you are using and the type and degree of input from each source.
   - Let them see that defining the future is not an event but a process that will go on forever. Show them that putting the outside boundaries on the future gives everyone in the organization a framework within which to build the future.

4. Build people throughout the organization into the process.
   - If the future is described clearly in language that the employees can understand, they can see themselves there and describe what *they* will be doing in the future: how they will work and interact within their own department, with management, with each other, with other departments, with customers, and with suppliers. If the employees cannot translate the company picture of the future into *their* future, you either need to define or communicate the future better.
   - Cascading the future down through the organization should be a structured process that funnels back up to senior management. This is an excellent test of the future state's integrity and of the communication system. It also starts the process of moving people from the present, by getting people throughout the company to begin to *own* the future.

As a movie channel, *HBO* on cable television provides a constant barrage of movies, from new to old, good to bad. In the past few years, they have added several features in addition to the movies. One that is of interest to students of change is the half-hour-to hour-long segments wrapped around a movie, showing how the movie was made. People are fascinated with these shows. Seeing how the director decided to put in this scene instead of that one, how the actors thought out their interpretation of the scene, and the way the wardrobe people chose the clothes of the period are of tremendous interest to the audience. They want to see "how" the movie was made. It enriches their understanding and appreciation of the film itself. HBO understands the change process, and how to get people to watch and watch again!

Supporting the Delta State

People need help getting through the delta. They need to know that the company understands their difficulties and is ready to provide them with support, encouragement, and help. A key way to convey that message is through the communication system.

As people move through the delta, they need constant reminders of why they left the old way and where they are going. Now is when the vision statement hung on the wall or printed on the back of their business card is valuable. Now the future state symbol is backed up by a plan they can see. It truly is a representation of something real—the future.

Two-way communication is critical in the delta. Even people who readily left the present and rushed toward the future experience difficulties in the delta. Because the future is never fully defined and changes daily, many people who hurried to it suddenly find it is a future they do not like. Some still feel that they signed up for a future that looks good, but the change process seems to be going on forever. Resistance flares. The delta is defeating them. They wish the whole change would just go away!

Those who were hesitant, afraid, or reluctant in the first place will often find themselves wishing they could go back. They question why they decided to go forward at all. Their original fears and concerns become justified. It is even worse than they expected it to be.

The communication system must have a process for expressing those fears, concerns, confusion, and the feelings of anger or sadness that are part of leaving the old way, living in the delta, and moving toward a shifting, ill-defined future.

This is when it is critical to provide people with ways to say:

- I am angry.
- I am confused.
- I don't think we're going in the right direction.
- I wish we didn't have to do this.

This is also the time to grieve for the old, familiar, comfortable way that will cease to exist. This is the time for funerals. Every society and civilization includes funerals as an important part of their rituals. Funerals exist because the living need an opportunity to say good-bye. Letting go of the present is painful. Remember, the present provided a sense of security. Even if people recognized its inadequacies and flaws, at least they knew where the boundaries were, what the rules were. The forms people used, chairs they sat on, and people they had lunch with were the context of their work. As these things change and as more and more of them change faster and faster, it is hard to leave them all. It helps if people can say good-bye.

In Chapter 4 you saw how Helene Curtis provided an opportunity for people to say good-bye to an old manufacturing system. *Moen Faucet* also said good-bye to some behaviors that had worked very well in the old culture, but would not work in the future. They sponsored a series of Employee Involvement Conferences. These carefully constructed days mixed people from all the Moen locations, from every department and management, salaried and hourly employees. Bruce Carbonari, the president of Moen, attended each session. The purpose of the session was to define the future and commit to leaving the present.

After the future state of employee involvement had been defined it was not difficult to go back and identify the current behaviors that would not go into the future with the Moen employees. These behaviors were written down on 3-by-5 cards and discussed at length. Suddenly, in the midst of that discussion, the door to the conference room swung open dramatically, and there stood a bishop dressed in all his regalia. He was carrying a small casket and went among the group collecting those cards. He gave a eulogy and extolled the virtues of behaviors that had worked in the past, making Moen a strong, successful company. He pointed out that some of these behaviors were not going into the future with Moen. He took them away. Lifting up the casket, he turned and left as dramatically as he had entered. The behaviors were gone. From that point on, whenever anyone behaved in an "old" way, they were reminded that that was not appropriate. That behavior was buried!

Clearly, communication regarding the change cannot be left to chance. Because it is such an important vehicle for making change happen it must be comprehensive, integrated, and varied.

Comprehensive

As you have read, at each stage in the change process there are key messages that must be delivered and certain key rules about how to deliver those messages. Because everyone in the organization does not move at the same pace, at any point in time some people knock at the door of the future, others stumble awkwardly through the delta, and others cling fiercely to the present. Therefore, the messages needed by each of these groups must be out in the organization simultaneously.

Integrated

Since major transformational change is comprised of a variety of different changes, the messages about each subset of changes must be integrated with the other changes. Remember the fishbone diagram in Chapter 5. The test of an effective communication plan is whether every employee from the vice president of logistics to the clerk in accounts receivable can go home and explain to his or her family what changes are being made and how they fit together.

Varied

- Let's put out a newsletter!
  OK, but some people do not learn best by reading. Even those who do can only read so many newsletters, and there are at least five major changes going on in the company.
- Let's have the president make a video. We'll send a copy to every employee at home!
  OK, but what the president says in his video may not be the same thing that the employee's manager said earlier in the day. Which message will the employee believe?

- Let's give everyone a laminated card with the company vision and guiding behaviors on it. They can carry it in their pocket or wallet and we'll give prizes to those people who can say what's on the card without looking!

  OK, but is there a penalty for *not* having the card with you? Is there any way to check whether people who are good at memorizing *understand* what the words mean? Any way to check if the people who carry the card *believe* what is on the card?

All of these ideas are effective communication tactics. The point is that any one of them, alone, may or may not work. It may work for some people and not for others. It may work for a period of time, and then become ineffective.

This is where the creativity and sensitivity of the change agents becomes a real asset.

Targets of change never exist in isolation. They have families and friends, people who are affected by what affects the targets. One of the best ways to help targets is to give them the tools to communicate what is happening when they go home at night. Many companies are sending letters to the employee's home, addressed to the whole family, explaining the change, discussing its impact on the company, the target, and the community as a whole.

E-mail is a wonderful tool of communication. The message from the president can come directly to every employee on the system in an instant. It can immediately be backed up by support messages from the cascade of management down to the target's manager. Most important, it is easy to set up a response system, asking targets to send e-mail messages back with their comments and questions, signed or unsigned.

One company handed every employee a little red plastic flag mounted on a dowel rod in a little wooden platform. Any time employees had questions about the changes going on they could set that flag on their desk, work station, or machine. A sponsor (manager) who spotted that flag stopped and answered the questions or got an answer to the employee within 24 hours.

DESIGNING THE ROLLOUT

Designing an effective communication plan is very hard. It must be carefully constructed by the change agents with the help of communication experts inside or outside the company. The change agents, however, do not deliver the messages. To ensure the success of the plan, they design an effective strategy for getting the message out. They write the speeches. The sponsors deliver them.

Targets of change do *not* want to hear about the changes from the human resources department. If the implementation team's primary change agents are not their direct manager and manager's manager, they do *not* want to hear about the changes from this team.

They *do* want to hear about the changes from their manager, from their manager's manager, and from the head of the company. They check for consistency in those messages. Targets want to hear news from people in direct contact with them. They want to bring questions directly to people they know and trust. In this way, targets become a link in the communication cascade and partners in the change process.

In almost every ongoing company change today, the targets of the change are not just the front-line workers. Everyone is affected by these major, transformational changes. Even the most senior management want to hear about the changes from the internal cascade. They do not want to hear about it from the management consultant or read about it in the *Wall Street Journal*. Every target,

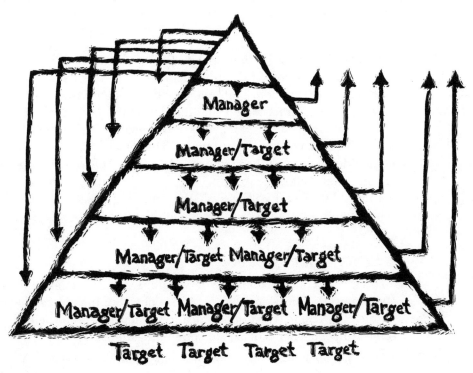

Figure 8.1
The Communication Cascade

from the vice president of finance to the accounts payable clerk, wants to hear about the changes from his or her manager. They would like to hear it from *all* the management, all the way up the ladder. Those messages need to come directly from the layer above as well as from the very top. Then they need vehicles to respond and communicate up and across (See Figure 8.1).

Implementation of an effective communication plan means the targets are informed about the changes from the person directly above them, who was informed from the person directly above him or her, etc. At the same time, every target is getting information about the change from the president and senior management through meetings, videos, newsletters, and small group get-togethers. This multiple process means the targets get the information in a variety of ways and from a variety of sources. If the messages are inconsistent, the change is in serious jeopardy. If the messages come from only one source or are sent through only one vehicle, the change is in serious jeopardy.

Therefore a communication plan must include not just the messages to be communicated and the communication vehicles. It must also lay out the process of getting those messages to the targets from two sources: the traditional cascade of management, whether a pyramid or a matrix design, and the top levels of management.

Larkin and Larkin in their book, *Communicating Change,* show through research studies that information shared by the direct supervisor is respected and believed. Therefore each person's direct supervisor must be empowered with the change information that the targets need. Larkin and Larkin call the supervisor the "privileged receiver of information" who then shares that information with his or her direct reports. This makes it critical to pass that information down through the organizational ranks. Therefore change agents on the communication team must build into their communication plan both the information vehicles that will cascade the change messages down and an effective accountability system for ensuring that the cascade does its work well.

A NEVER-ENDING TASK

To their credit, many companies are beginning to understand the importance of communication in major change. At the outset of the project they create Communication Teams. The Communication Teams should be held accountable for three critical elements of a good communication system:

1. A rich and creative mix of methods for sending the messages about the change.

2. A process to ensure that the cascade of management knows its role in the communication process and fulfills its responsibilities.
3. Careful construction and evaluation of the messages to be sure they address answers to these critical questions from targets:
    - Why are we changing?
        - Is it because management thinks we have been stupid?
        - Is it because of things beyond our control?
    - Do we know what the future looks like?
    - What happens if we don't change?
    - How long do we have?
    - What is the company going to do to help us get through the change?
    - What have we learned from our past attempts at change that will help us get through this one?
    - Is everything changing? It sure seems like it!
    - What is my role in the future?
    - What is my role in the delta?

Communication Teams are as important 18 months into the change as they are at the beginning. So they must also be prepared to hang in for the duration, and the sponsors must be prepared to support the long lifespan required.

II. REAL WORLD *Treetop Manufacturing Company*

CHARLIE

Charlie and his team had been moving pretty fast. The basic framework of the future was outlined. The department would make a major investment in new systems and processes. Concurrent engineering would be the foundation of the department's operation. They would use Quality Function Deployment, involving suppliers, customers, manufacturing, sales, and a variety of users and contributors. The new CAD system and the use of QFD would go a long way toward shortening design time. The emphasis on design for manufacturability would greatly shorten time to market.

The whole department understood all of this. The team had shared the design with them over the months it had evolved. Many people in the department gave input into the design and several were already heading in the right direction. Four of the engineers went to the vendor's school to learn the new CAD system. The whole department was scheduled for a Concurrent Engineering Methodology seminar next month.

Charlie and the team were beginning to get a sense of the overarching elements of the changes they were initiating. As things moved along they were also getting a sense of the targets' issues and concerns. At their meeting this morning, Sam, who was serving as the change management expert, suggested that they put some structure around their change efforts.

"We've been doing a lot of sharing and communicating with people in the department, but it has been pretty haphazard," said Sam. "From what we know about good change management strategies, that's probably not a good idea. I suggest we lay out a better plan for ensuring that all the information people need gets to everyone at the right time."

"But isn't it too late?" Jane asked. "We're three months into this process and everyone knows what we're doing and why. We don't need to go back, do we? That sounds like a lot of unnecessary work."

"I have done a little informal testing," Sam answered. "I've been asking a few simple questions of people in the department whenever I get a chance. 'Why are we changing? What will we look like two years from now? Do you think we really need to do all of this? Can you see a place for yourself in the future of Treetop's engineering department?' I don't like the answers I've been getting, Jane. There is a lot of confusion, mistrust, and apprehension out there. I think we should start from scratch and see if we can ease some of that tension."

"What do you propose?" Charlie asked.

"First, I've written a memo explaining why we have to change and what would happen if we didn't. It outlines the framework of the future we put together and fits the framework into the ongoing changes throughout the rest of the company. I recommend we get John Shane to co-sign this memo, Charlie. That's not meant to undermine or diminish your authority, but it sends the message that this change is larger than just engineering and that even in the engineering department you have John's sponsorship behind you. From what I have been hearing, the most bothersome feeling is that we are denigrating the way things are currently run. People see these changes as a direct criticism of them. We have to show them that the problems are in the processes and tools, not in them."

"That sure fits what Sarah's survey team unearthed," said Tom. "People are feeling threatened. Many of them seem to feel all this change is because we think they have been goofing off or didn't care. That's not true. We know they have tried hard to get good work done around here, but our research has shown that our processes and tools frequently got in their way."

"I think it is critical that we get that message across," said Sam. "I also think we better keep communication going both ways. As the next step in our communication plan, I've prepared a little questionnaire that will go out with the memo. It has the questions I've been asking people already and a place for more questions, gripes, and issues. I'll set up a box next to the coffee machines for people to drop off the questionnaire. They can sign it or leave it anonymously, but we'll promise a response by early next week. Let's do two responses: a written response and a department-wide meeting.

"Then, I'd like to work with Georgette Dunlap, the communication person in marketing, to design a little logo for the Engineering Partnership. Put up a few signs, and maybe come up with a few handouts, stickers, pens, and so on to keep the whole change in front of people.

"The most important thing is that we bring in the supervisors before any of this goes out to the department. They are targets, too, so I would like to deal with them first. That way, they become sponsors who are more prepared and informed. It is critical that the information in this memo match what the sponsor cascade is saying about these change issues."

"Wow," Jane exclaimed. "That sounds like a lot of work, Sam, but I trust you. You're the expert. What do you need from us?"

The team bent their heads together and began to flesh out the plan and their roles.

SARAH

What had once been a simple conference room was rapidly becoming "Change Headquarters." The 100 Percent Solution team had taken over the third floor conference room. One wall was filled with a giant fishbone diagram. Another, from floor to ceiling, contained the company's organization chart with designations of sponsor, targets, and change agent assigned to the various job functions. Three computers and their accompanying printers, a copier, a scanner, and a wastebasket full of emptied coffee cups, soda cans, and pizza crusts were all evidence of the work they had been doing.

Today the team was meeting to review the work done by the Communication Subcommittee. Like the Engineering Partnership team, this overarching change team made a commitment to design a well thought out, comprehensive communication strategy. Along with the Engineering Partnership team, they had learned a critical lesson over the past few months, integration. They knew their communication strategy had to incorporate what the engineering group was doing. So before coming out with their recommendations they had met with the engineering change team and integrated their change plan *and* their change messages into the overall change strategy.

Sarah was not at this critical meeting. She had to attend to a different communication task. Charlie and Sarah had had a long conversation about Keith Bailer. Charlie recounted his lunch with the vice president of manufacturing and the fears and concerns that Keith had expressed. After several long hours of thinking, she and Charlie came up with a strategy.

"Keith's concerns and fears are real, and from his perspective they appear to be justified," said Sarah. "We need Keith's sponsorship for all these changes, but we forgot that before he can be a sponsor, he needs to deal with his issues and feelings as a target. That's what he was doing at lunch."

Sarah's strategy for the next step was simple. "If Keith has issues and fears around these changes, we need to get them out on the table. But we are just the change agents, Charlie. John is Keith's sponsor. They need to have a conversation, but let's be in the room with them. Let's be sure the conversation gets at the issues Keith shared with you, and help John and Keith keep the issues within the framework of the change process. We need to structure the meeting so John sends the right messages to Keith about the future and the need for change. Keith needs to know that his issues are both logical and appropriate from his perspective. This is a critical communication opportunity."

Today, Sarah was sitting in a smaller conference room down the hall with Keith. Sitting next to her was John Shane, and across the table, next to Keith, sat Charlie. Sarah watched, listened, and occasionally restated things said in that meeting. At times she nudged the two key players along, pointing out how their issues fit into the framework of the change process. It was working. John and Keith were really communicating! Keith was taking the opportunity to air his issues. John was listening, and because of the coaching she had given him, refraining from jumping all over Keith. Instead, he restated the need for all these changes. He validated Keith's role in getting Treetop to where it was today and commiserated with him on how difficult it was to continue to grow rapidly the way they were structured today. He sympathized, too, with the fuzzy definition of Keith's role in the future and admitted that if he were Keith, that would be pretty frightening.

Sarah talked less and listened more. She could hear the results of her efforts as a change agent. Because of her and Charlie, Keith had been able to express his resistance to all these changes. Equally important, because of her coaching of John, he was able to play out the role of an effective sponsor, acknowledging Keith's resistance and working with him to deal with it. John was a good sponsor. He had been an eager student, willing to be coached. Now the results of their efforts together were playing out in front of her.

"This is going to work," she thought. "Keith's fears and concerns are not going to go away with one meeting, but we are on the right path. The right players are in place, doing what they are supposed to do. This isn't *my* change anymore. John and Keith are taking ownership. We just might pull this off." She smiled to herself and turned her attention back to the meeting.

III. TOOLS FOR CHANGE

PLANNING A COMMUNICATION SYSTEM

If change management is a methodology, it requires a rigorous discipline of planning and execution. That planning is best seen in the need to lay out a blueprint for the communication strategy. The blueprint must include effective communication vehicles at all three stages of the change process: the present, delta, and future.

It must identify what messages need to be sent at each stage to each unique group of targets. Those groups might be by function, geographic region, position in the organizational hierarchy, or all of the above.

How the messages get delivered, by whom and when, cannot be left to chance. The change agents cannot assume that feedback will occur. They *can* assume there will be reactions to the messages. But any reactions shared by two or more employees standing around the coffeepot that stop the minute a manager walks by is a problem. Getting those people at the coffeepot to share their comments and observations is critical, and the change agents have to design ways to get that information.

Use this form to identify the key elements of the communication plan and develop the tactics required to implement it.

Stage	Message	Audience	Delivery Method	Presenter	Timing	Feedback Process
The Present						
The Delta						
The Future						

9
The Learning System

People make choices about whether or not to change based on two key variables:

1. Do I *want* to change?
2. Do I *know how* to change and be successful in the future state?

You have already read about the issues surrounding people's desire to change and how to help them make an informed choice about changing.

Many issues also surround knowing *how* to change. You can deal with these issues by providing people with the knowledge, skills, and tools to move into and live in the future. That is the job of education and training. Built correctly, education and training become the foundation for a constantly learning environment that will support ongoing change.

Education and training are becoming important resources in companies' efforts to change. Billions of dollars are spent on training in the United States alone by companies that recognize its importance in the change process. Much of that money is wasted, however. People don't use the training. They don't seem to learn what they need to know. They resent the time training takes and treat training as a nuisance to be avoided if at all possible. Effective, efficient education and training must be used within the context and understanding of the change process.

The United States will not convert to the *metric system*. Despite incredible efforts (and funding) by the government, the people of this country refuse to change. There are many reasons for this successful resistance. A primary cause was lack of motivation: people could not see the need to change. The country's attitude of superiority and a feeling that the rest of the world should copy the United States set people up to resist. Why wasn't the rest of the world changing to this country's system?

There was another major reason the metric system never 'took' in the United States. People did not know *how* to use it! Signs went up on highways showing miles and kilometers to the next town but people didn't see the relationship between the two measures. Like learning a foreign language, learning metric required connecting those kilometers to the miles and having a sense of how far a kilometer is. People could not do it! The only people who understood the metric system were the scientists, people who dealt with foreign products and needed to know, and elementary-school children and their teachers. All that money spent changing signs, food labels, toiletries, and factory parts was wasted. The large majority of people, who didn't want to change in the first place, didn't really know what that information meant. So everyone not providing products for other countries ignored it. Now metric is dead as the standard for this country.

THE DIFFERENCE

First, everyone needs a common definition of the key elements in the learning system: education and training.

- **Education**—providing an overview and an understanding of how the newly required skills and activities fit into the framework of the future state.
- **Training**—providing opportunities to learn, practice, and apply the specific skills and activities required in the future state.

A one-day seminar on Design for Manufacturability is usually a combination of education and training, but its primary emphasis is on education. As a result of attending that seminar, the participants should be able to explain Design for Manufacturability and identify its key components and the skills required for it to work. They should also understand the impact it will have on the various populations of targets—engineering, manufacturing, vendors, and customers. That is the education part. The participants may have some training included: practice in charting and analysis and actually using some formats in class.

However, the participants seldom can go back to their company and install a Design for Manufacturability process as the result of one seminar. They lack certain skills and tools, and they are not even sure how to use the tools they did get. Moving the participants from understanding to proficiency will require additional hours of training.

A change management strategy for education and training must differentiate between the two. Education comes before training. It is built into the communication strategy. It is strongly emphasized as people leave the current state and move into the delta. Indeed, it is vital to their ability to make an informed decision to leave the current state.

Training comes after people have had an education regarding the future state, how it will look, and what the implications are for achieving the future. With models in place of the skills, tools, and behaviors required in the future, they can start to practice using those resources (8.1).

	Current State	**Delta**	**Future State**
Education	Heavy		Light
Training	Light	Heavy	Heavier

Figure 9.1
Strategy for Education and Training

CRITICAL FACTORS TO BUILD INTO A LEARNING SYSTEM PLAN

To ensure a successful learning system strategy, the change agents must pay particular attention to four core elements of effective learning:

1. Sequence
2. Design
3. Resources
4. Planning

Sequence

In most changing companies the education and training required for change is done either at the wrong time or in the wrong order. Timing is a critical part of the plan for new learning.

If you want to learn how to race a car, you need to know how to drive one first. Equally important, you have to want to race that car. Your teacher has to do two key things:

First: Create an environment where you *want* to race.

Then: Teach you how to race in the right sequence of steps, starting with "This is a steering wheel!"

There are hundreds of thousands of employees sitting in classrooms every day who do not benefit from the class time because they are not ready to learn. Some of them don't have a context for the learning: "What does this have to do with me?" Others don't want to learn: "This is stupid. I feel threatened." Still others are being taught poorly: "What does it mean to 'take the apex?' I just want to know when to hit the brakes."

The rollout of education and training programs must be from the top down. Each level of the organization will have different programs, designed for its own needs. People know from past experience that if they learn a new skill, behavior, or application of a new tool and the management cascade above them is not familiar with it, it will not be supported. In fact, too often in the past, employees who applied what they learned in training were criticized and discouraged if management did not understand what they were doing. People learn quickly from those negative experiences. So, in the seminar that introduces the new computer system to track customer order status, one of the first questions some brave student always asks is, "Have our managers been through this training?" What the class really wants to know is, "Do our managers know what you, the teacher, are about to teach us? Will they support the application of this new learning? Will I get in trouble if I try it? Will I get in trouble if I *don't* try it?"

Education and training cannot be an afterthought. The identification of who needs to know what, when they need to know it, and how it will be taught must be built into the very early stages of the change planning. The resulting plan will be modified and adapted over the life of the project. However, it needs to be designed early enough so sufficient, timely resources are allocated to make it happen.

Design

Instructional design is a critical asset. Instructional designers must build into their methodology a sensitivity to the target resistance issues that will affect the learner.

Make Sure They Are Ready To Learn

The targets of change who must learn a new skill or behavior are adults. They will learn only if they choose to learn. Management can force them to attend a training class; *they* will decide if they are going to get any value out of it. People should walk into a training situation eager to learn. The trainer cannot assume that people are willing to learn, however. The training design should test the participant's willingness to learn at the front end of the session.

Learners must know why they are in the training class. They need to review the changes that are taking place and be able to place this new skill, behavior, or application of a tool into the context of those changes. They need to understand before they start the learning process why *they* are in the room. Are there others they think should have this learning in addition to them, or instead of them?

Before launching into the specific learning experience, the instructor or instructions need to lay out what they will learn and what previous knowledge or experiences will form the basis for that learning. Students should also see how the learning experience is designed, how they are going to be judged in the session and afterward, and what the consequences are for successfully (or unsuccessfully) learning the information presented.

Select the Right Learning Tool

Often the best tool for learning is not a seminar or a training class. Think about what the learners need to know, how well they need to know it, and what they need to do as a result of that learning. Is this learning best accomplished in a seminar, in one-on-one sessions, as computer-based training, or with job aids such as check lists, pamphlets, or charts? Choose the best options for the learner's needs.

Use the Learner's Perspective

Professional training designers know that one key element in a successful design is to put the learning format into a frame of reference that makes sense to the learner. People in Information Systems who design training for people on the shop floor, or engineers who design training for the sales and marketing people, often ignore this key element of successful design. Don't!

If you want the learners to understand you and the points you are making, you need to speak their language. Put the information into a perspective that makes sense to them and use stories from their work. Use examples, case studies, and exercises that relate *directly* to their work, their experiences, and their way of interpreting the world.

Protect the Learner

It has happened to everyone; no one likes it. It might have been in the third grade, a college statistics class, or a management training session last year. It might have been in all those situations. You looked stupid in front of your peers.

If you allow training to be designed to let that happen or if you allow training facilitators to embarrass learners, you deserve a failed change. If you allow those things to happen, you probably *will* have a failed change, at least for one target.

Resources

There are excellent people in the field of education and training. If you are not an expert, go get one. There's a good chance you have someone right inside your company in the human resources department. How do you know if they are any good? Listen for them to tell you what you have just read here and more. If they do not know these things, get someone else. If they do know these things, make them a major player on your change team. They will work with you to build a strong education and training program. They can also design and develop courses and support materials, or find the best materials already designed and ready for you to bring inhouse.

Planning

The serious change agent knows that a key element in managing change is the ability to plan. This is true for all three change management tool systems: communication, learning, and rewards and reinforcements.

Initial planning should include identification of all key targets. You can easily use this information to develop spreadsheets that identify the education and training elements needed for each target population. Ask the following questions:

- *Who* needs to learn *what*?
- What are the *issues* that will affect the learning?
- *How* will the learning occur?
- *When* will it occur?
- *How will the change agent know if the learning experience has been successful?*

This planning tool can then be married into a project plan or built into a critical path or pert chart as an integral part of the change process.

Note that the questions to be addressed are not just the who, what, when, and where of traditional training plans. The issues surrounding resistance, sponsorship, and change agent requirements are carefully built into the plan so they can be addressed in the design and delivery of the training.

As important as the learning experience is the need to hold the learner accountable for applying new skills or behavior. Knowledgeable training designers

Learners	Learning	Issues
Senior Management	• Overview of the system. New ways of thinking about information that is synthesized, coming to them from subordinates with recommendations and, in many cases, actions already taken. • New ways of managing—getting out of people's way as they play "what if" in small groups. • Encouraging risk.	• Few models in their peer group. • Little direct incentive for them to change. Don't see the need to change, just expect the people to do what is asked of them. • Several may not be able to learn enough in time.
Middle Management	• Overview of the system. Redefines parameters of decision making responsibility. • How to use data for long-range projections and development of strategies, not for immediate problem solving.	• Few models in their peer group. • Little direct incentive for them to change. Don't see the need to change, just expect the people to do what is asked of them. • Several may not be able to learn enough in time. • Some may not be able to learn these skills at all.

First-Line Management	• Overview of the system.
	• Detail:
	  Pertinent Modules
	   Charting
	   Analysis
	   Team Work
	   Design of Experiments
	   Coaching
	   Training
		• Few models in their peer group.
		• Little direct incentive for them to change. Don't see the need to change, just expect the people to do what is asked of them.
		• Several may not be able to learn enough in time.
		• Some may not be able to learn these skills at all.
		• Many fear their job will be going away.

Professionals/ Technical	• Overview of the system.
	• Detail:
	  Pertinent Modules
	   Charting
	   Analysis
	   Team Work
	   Design of Experiments
		• Do not trust management to change their behavior.
		• Do not have knowledge of and trust of other departments.

Learners	Learning	Issues

Clerical	• Overview of the system.
	• Detail:
	    Pertinent Modules
	    Charting
	    Analysis
	    Team Work
	    Design of Experiments
		• Fear they will not be able to learn
		• Fear they will not be allowed to really use these tools.
		• Do not see what is in it for them to learn.

Shop Floor	• Overview of the system.
	• Detail:
	    Pertinent Modules
	    Charting
	    Communication
	    Team Work
	    Design of Experiments
	    Analysis
		• Fear they will not be able to learn.
		• Fear they will not be allowed to really use these tools.
		• Do not see what is in it for them to learn.

Union Leadership	• Overview of the system. • Redefinition of the role of management and the workforce.	• Do not see the advantage for their membership. • Do not see the advantage for them.

Figure 9.2

Education and Training Plan for the Implementation of a Client Server Manufacturing System with a Relational Database

know that this is a critical ingredient in all training. If organizational change requires change in people's skills and actions, then a method of measuring those changes must be built into the training program.

These elements can be addressed in a simple paper-and-pencil chart or an elaborate project plan.

From this in-depth analysis of each learner group, the education and training requirements and the who/what/where/when can be built. Most important, the performance criteria that determine whether the participant has successfully accomplished the learning is embedded in the plan.

AN INTEGRATED STRATEGY

The planning, design, and identification of what should be taught, to whom it should be taught, and when and how the learning loop is closed all need to come together into an overall learning strategy. Many companies invest in an

Learners	Delivery Vehicle	Date/Time/Place	Measurable Result
Senior Management	• Seminar • One-on-one meetings • Presentations at staff meetings		• Performance Objectives • Business Measurements Behavior Measurements
Middle Management	• Seminar • Workshops for practice and reinforcement • One-on-one coaching sessions		• Performance Objectives • Business Measurements Behavior Measurements
First-Line Management	• Seminar • Workshops for practice and reinforcement • One-on-one coaching sessions		• Performance Objectives • Business Measurements Behavior Measurements
Professionals/ Technical	• Seminar • Workshops for practice and reinforcement • One-on-one coaching sessions		• Performance Objectives • Business Measurements Behavior Measurements
Clerical	• Seminar • Workshops for practice and reinforcement • One-on-one coaching sessions		• Performance Objectives • Business Measurements Behavior Measurements
Shop Floor	• Seminar • Workshops for practice and reinforcement • One-on-one coaching sessions		• Performance Objectives • Business Measurements Behavior Measurements
Union Leadership	• Seminar • Ongoing discussions at all meetings		• Identified changes in language and demands

Figure 9.3
Education and Training Project Plan

educational workshop here, a training program there. But they are not willing to expend the resources needed for a comprehensive strategic approach. While companies are getting good at paying lip service to the need for training, very few really understand what that means. Companies who have embraced change management do understand.

Compaq Computer Corporation knows what it takes to be competitive. It has leveraged that knowledge to catapult ahead of its competitors and to grow at incredible speed. One of the things Compaq does best is manage change. It understands that change is a constant and that the company that can change rapidly, with minimum pain, will be the company that comes out on top. To accomplish this, Compaq is teaching itself to respond to market changes, tolerate a high level of chaos, and live with delta conditions as a constant. That learning is occurring throughout the company. Compaq knew that putting a course on "Change Management" into the human resource training catalog was not the way to teach people these critical lessons.

Instead, Compaq wrapped the learning opportunities around key business initiatives. As the company began to reengineer its logistics operations and introduce major changes in its information management technology, it provided the change agents, sponsors, and targets with exposure to change management principles as they required it.

Early in the project, change agents needed a deep understanding of the critical elements of change and how to deal with them. So they went to workshops and seminars and brought their change project with them. They sat down together and applied the new learning in a just-in-time work setting.

That learning was supported throughout the life of the project by a group of "Change Consultants," people in Compaq who showed an early aptitude for understanding and applying change principles and received additional training and support. These Change Consultants were available to the change agents as they struggled to define the future, analyze the present, and plan the delta.

Sponsors needed two things early in the change:
1. A broad-brush overview of the change process and how it would affect their project.
2. An understanding of the roles of sponsors, change agents, and targets.

They didn't need to spend days and days on this effort; some only needed a few hours. The learning from those sessions was supported and encouraged by the Change Consultants over the next few years.

As the project unfolded, however, sponsors needed continuous reinforcement and on-the-job coaching. This was best done by the Change Consultants in hallway conversations, during lunch, in one-on-one meetings, and in reminders at staff meetings. The lessons were reinforced in the executive and management development opportunities the sponsors had over the life of the project. Compaq Europe developed an outstanding Executive Leadership Seminar. The series taught management to think into the future, showed them how to apply new theories to create a learning organization, and reinforced the need to sponsor the change *to* a learning organization.

Targets needed to know how to cope with and understand the change process. They also needed reassurance by understanding what they had a right to expect from change agents and sponsors, and understanding that their feelings and concerns were normal and natural under the circumstances. This reduced stress in the delta and built a high tolerance for the delta.

Everyone at Compaq who was affected by change was offered the opportunity to gain this knowledge. As they moved through the delta and learned new skills, technologies, and behaviors, knowledge of the change process was embedded in that learning.

II. REAL WORLD *Treetop Manufacturing Company*

CHARLIE

Money was getting tight. For the past six months the change effort had been draining resources throughout Treetop, especially in engineering. The demand for some customized work for a very special customer had required Charlie to make a choice: either slow down the change effort or add resources. He knew the cost of slowing down the momentum he had begun. Besides, his changes were now integral to the overarching changes throughout Treetop. Other departments were waiting for his group to get their new design strategies in place so they could begin to knock down some of the walls that had been in the way. His people were anxious for the new systems and tools. There was energy in the department that he did not want to diffuse.

He had hired a lot of extra help, both permanent and temporary, to support the ongoing needs of the department while these changes were taking place. It was beginning to show on the bottom line. Charlie was running out of money. Besides that, business was down this quarter. At the senior staff meetings, Susan Sullivan, the head of finance, was starting to talk about belt tightening.

That meant the proposal in front of him was about to give him an ulcer. Jane, from his change team, had put together a special task force to design the training needs for the department over the next twelve months. She asked several key members of the department, some senior, experienced people and several brand-new engineers as well as the training director from the human resources department to help. The resulting report was impressive. Jane certainly understood the importance of training and its place in the change process. The rationale for each education and training requirement was carefully thought out. The resource requirements had been identified and costed out.

That was the problem, the cost! It was *very* impressive. Charlie's head began to pound as he looked at the bottom-line figure. Months and months ago, when they began this change process, they knew they would have to do some training. It hadn't seemed like a big deal. Although they had built it in as a line item in their planning budget, the team didn't know how to allocate any costs to this item, so they threw in a few thousand dollars and forgot about it. Those few thousand dollars were not going to be enough. Not by a long shot!

As Charlie studied the report, his admiration for the work of the committee begin to turn to anger. Those folks had better start living in the real world! This was ridiculous. All this training would be great, but it wasn't necessary. They would just have to cut this plan. This was an engineering department, not a graduate school. If people needed more, they could just go outside and sign up for courses at the college in town. Working up a full head of steam, he reached for the phone and angrily punched in Jane's extension.

When Jane arrived at Charlie's office, he waved the report in her face and began to describe his appraisal of her team's work. Unrealistic, pie in the sky, cadillac were some of the terms he used. Jane's first reaction was to be defensive. She waited with diminishing patience for Charlie's tirade to die down so she could lash out. How dare he accuse her group of being unrealistic! It was Charlie who had been insisting that they pay attention to the human issues involved in this change. It was those human issues that had driven the training plan into its length and expense. It wasn't very expensive to teach people the technical skills and knowledge they would need. It was all that "soft" stuff that was going to take so much time and money. Charlie better not forget that.

Of course, Charlie hadn't. As he ranted and raved at Jane his tirade began to lose steam. Charlie started listening to himself and heard the same flaw in his logic that Jane was hearing. Of course they needed to educate and train at this level. Of course that was exactly what he asked the committee to design. He just hadn't realized it would be this expensive. Charlie calmed down. He had what he had asked for. He had what was needed. The problem was that the committee did not know, while it was working, that there was a resource consideration. That was Charlie *and* Jane's fault.

Now they had a choice. They could throw the report out, put in some bare-bones skill training and cross their fingers.

"No," Jane said, reaching for Charlie's copy of the report. "We have all come too far and done too many things right to see it all go up in smoke over improper or poor training. That's a risk I'm not willing to take, Charlie. The committee will go back to the drawing board. We won't back off on who needs what training and education. We will take a long hard look at training design and delivery resources and requirements. I'll bet there's a lot of slop in here. Remember, we weren't looking at the budget constraints when we designed this. Give us another week. We'll work on it. What *can* you live with? How much do we need to carve out of this plan?"

"I'm really worried about our resource requirements, Jane," Charlie said. "Cut 35 percent out for the rest of this year and 25 percent out for next year. Do you think you can do that without compromising the plan?"

"Don't know," said Jane. "Give us a few days and we'll get back to you."

During the coming week, Charlie didn't see much of Jane and her group. He thought a lot about them, though. He kept remembering one of the line items in the plan, management development. The plan had talked about the need for management to learn new skills and techniques if the changes were going to work. Charlie and his direct reports were to be scheduled for several training sessions on coaching, team leadership, and conflict resolution. Charlie resented the fact that Jane and the committee felt that he needed training in those areas. After all, he had been manager of this department for over five years. He was a good manager. Why did he need to go to a training session? Besides, those sessions were stupid. Lots of role plays and discussions about 'feelings!'

He kept remembering the meeting he and Sarah witnessed between Keith and John Shane, though. John was outstanding in his ability to listen, draw Keith out, address his issues and fears, and reassure him without compromising the changes. Together, they reached agreement on what needed to be done, and it was evident that Keith felt a lot better when the meeting was over. Charlie remembered his own meeting with Keith. He had learned a lot from Keith, but had done little, if anything, to make Keith feel better. Maybe he could learn from those training sessions, but he would expect them to disappear from the list of recommendations when Jane's group came back. After all, they were not the most important thing; they were one of those "nice-to-haves."

One week later Jane and the committee asked Charlie for an hour of his time. They came into his office with a flip chart and a new report they proudly handed to him. "Charlie, we were really proud of our first effort,"

Duane Jamison said. Duane was obviously the spokesperson for the committee. He was one of the most senior engineers on Charlie's staff. As far as Charlie knew, Duane hadn't learned anything new since about 1968.

"We studied the way to use education and training as a strong tool of the change process and built our plan around that concept. When Jane came and said we had to go back to the drawing board because of the cost, we were appalled. We didn't see how we could change it. It was too good. So we did not change it."

Charlie sat up straighter. What had they been up to for a week? What the hell was going on here?

"We looked at each learner group, what they needed to know and the issues surrounding that learning," continued Duane. "Those things are our reality. We can't change those. So we did not cut out any learner groups. We did not compromise what they need to learn and did not ignore any of the issues that will impact that learning, but we *did* meet your criteria of cutting cost. When we rolled up our sleeves we found out there are many ways to address those learning needs and issues. We have slashed 35 percent from the budget for the last quarter of this year and for next year as well. So we met your criteria and exceeded it by over 10 percent for all of next year, but we did it in the design and delivery areas, not in the learner need area."

Duane put up the flip chart and reviewed the learners, learner requirements, and learner issues. As he had indicated, they remained the same as in the original report. Then he moved to the next chart and there things looked different. "There are many ways to deliver training," Duane began. "We were lazy in our original work because we did not feel the need to be creative and careful. So at each juncture we picked the best or what we thought was the best, but Bob Milton, our training expert, was a great help. He showed us that with better identification of the knowledge and skill requirements, delivering the right training at the right time without spending extraordinary funds is much easier. We also got busy looking for creative ways to address the resource crunch. We found that our state has set aside monies for re-training workers. We made a few phone calls and found we are eligible for a *very* large chunk of that money. The grant application is on Jane's desk right now, and every indication is that the state will fund most of our training.

"Besides that, it turns out that the local college has recently re-designed all of its engineering courses. They're willing to work with us to develop a special certification course that our engineers can take on QFD. They will come here after hours to conduct the courses, charge us half the regular tuition rate, and give our people college credit. I'm going back to college, Charlie!" Duane laughed.

"The people we bought the CAD system from were willing to negotiate on their price for training. We offered them our resources to build into their training modules the issues of change and change management that we want to address. In return, they will cut their costs considerably. We also challenged their time frames. Bob Milton thought their course designs were cumbersome and the learning time could be cut considerably. They promised to work on that, and Bob will help.

"We found an internal way to spread the cost of this part of the project as well. You saw in our original presentation that there are considerable time and dollars allocated to an overview of the changes in engineering. We got to thinking that this part of the process might be best integrated into the education and training that Sarah and her people were doing. We talked to them, and they had already assumed that would happen and built it into their design. So we are going to work with them to make that happen.

"We're satisfied that everyone will learn what they need to learn, when they need it, in a way that will be valuable and useful for them. Besides that, we have challenged the training designers to be sure it will not be boring. It will not be dull. This is a great opportunity to have some fun and build some of the very changes we are striving for in terms of team work and integration within and between departments. Even the management development training promises to be fun, Charlie. If I can go back to college, even *you* can learn a new trick or two."

Charlie smiled. This team was pretty impressive. They were operating within the behaviors and characteristics of the future state. He'd have to go some way to keep up with them. He remembered his ranting and raving at Jane a week ago. Maybe some management training wouldn't be so bad, but it was hard to imagine role play being fun!

SARAH

Things were really starting to move! The communication plan was being implemented. The plan format was tacked up on the wall in the War Room, and as each communication action step was implemented, the team was checking it off with big red felt-tip pens.

The team was getting good feedback about their communication efforts. Management and workers were stopping them in the halls and after meetings to tell them how helpful it was to understand the changes, the reasons for them, and how they were going to happen.

Sarah had not been prepared for the strong response to John Shane's speeches on the shop floor. She accompanied John on several trips to plants where he held meetings with the workers, shutting down operations and spending at least an hour and a half with each group. The people were overwhelmingly positive in their response! They seemed very pleased that John had come to talk to them. They had a lot of questions about how a cellular operation would work and what kind of skills would be required of them. They seemed skeptical that management above them was going to change, but overall, they seemed excited and anxious to begin the process.

Flying back from the plant in Missouri one night, she and John tried to analyze the reaction they were getting.

"It's almost as if we had smothered those people under a blanket of repression and constraint," John reflected. "They know how to do their work. They seem to have a lot of ideas about how to make things better, improve quality, and cut costs. We just made it hard for them to share those ideas, so they stopped trying. It's incredible to me that after all those years of being treated that way, they still want to try. We better make sure this new way works, Sarah. Those people are counting on us!"

Sarah was determined that where the changes required people to behave in new ways or to do things with new tools, they would get all the help they needed. Her team, like Charlie's, had been busy working on a plan for education and training. It consisted of three parts:

1. An Overview
2. A Detailed Picture of the Future State
3. Specific Skill Training

An Overview

This was a two hour presentation they were using in the plants. It gave a picture of the future state and how each area of the company fit into it. It incorporated all the things Sarah's group had learned about effective communication of change. The combination of a slide show, speeches and handouts showed the reasons for changing, the consequences if Treetop didn't change, and a strong picture of what the company was doing to help people get through the delta.

A critical part of the two hours was the opportunity for people to ask questions and gain clarification. This was done by breaking people up into small, facilitated groups and giving them safe, anonymous ways to seek further information.

The success of this presentation inside the company gave Sarah's group an idea. They began to use this presentation with customers and with vendors who were going to be affected by the changes and change process at Treetop. So far, the presentations had been a great success!

A Detailed Picture of the Future State

As each plant, function, and operation began to understand the change, the next step was a carefully designed presentation that gave them an opportunity to understand the future state in much greater detail. Designed as a highly interactive, facilitated workshop, this step led the groups through a process to define the future of their own operation, work, and responsibilities. It helped them outline the degree of change required and the process for making those changes. The groups did this from their own frames of reference, but the design forced them to see that their operations, jobs, and even their views of the company could not continue without opening up to the issues and problems of other areas. This process was going far to reduce resistance to the changes because people were becoming involved in the solutions. They understood what changes needed to be made and the impact of making (or not making) those changes.

The results of these workshops were being reported through the special 100 Percent Solution newsletter that the communication group had developed. People were beginning to see a commonality from each workshop. Change was necessary! The changes that needed to be made had a common element too; *break down the old functional walls and let's get going!*

Specific Skill Training

The third step in the education and training plan was to slot specific target populations into the right skill and behavior training at the right time. Each training program had been carefully selected to be highly interactive and very targeted in the learning that occurred. All the programs had two common elements. At the front end of each lesson there was what Sarah's group called "the grounding." This was a brief review of the need to change, the future state, the impact of changing, and the impact of not changing. It reminded people why they were in the training environment and how this training fit into the larger picture of the future state.

At the beginning of each learning interaction there was also a clear presentation of the expectations of that interaction. What was the learner expected to be able to do as a result of this experience? How well was the learner expected to perform this skill or exhibit this behavior? What were the consequences of doing a good job? Of not doing a good job?

Sarah and her team now had one more huge wall chart filling the War Room: The Learning Plan. John Shane had stopped in this morning to say hello and congratulate the team members on the work they were doing. He walked slowly around the room, studying the charts and whistling softly to himself. Sarah and the team members who happened to be there watched him quietly.

Finally, he turned back to them with a thoughtful look on his face. "I had no idea when I asked you to head up this change what I was asking of you Sarah," he said. "I knew the changes we needed to make were big. I didn't think about how big the job of changing was. You people have done a great job. The process is evident on these walls. The result is evident out in the company. I'm feeling really good about where we're going and how we're going to get there, and I thank you for the job you are doing to make it happen."

It was only 5:30 when Sarah left the office that night. She was feeling good! She remembered her original fears and her confusion as this project had started, but John's speech today had confirmed what she had been feeling. Things *were* good!

III. TOOLS FOR CHANGE

THE LEARNING PLAN

There are many excellent training design models available. Use every aid that works for you. Just remember, the learner's issues surrounding the fact that the learning will result in a change *must* be addressed in the design of the learning experience.

Be careful not to design all the learning experiences using only one delivery method. The delivery method actually is dictated by several key elements:

- What needs to be learned.
- Who needs to learn.
- The learning circumstances:
    Time
    Dollars
    Geography

A good instructional designer will help you select the right learning delivery method and build you a strong learning experience.

Step One

Who are the learners, what do they need to learn, and what are their issues?

Learners	Learning	Issues
Senior Management		
Middle Management		
First-Line Management		
Professionals/Technical		
Clerical		
Shop Floor		
Union Leadership		

Step Two

How are those learning needs addressed?

Learners	Delivery Vehicle	Date/Time/Place	Measurable Result
Senior Management			
Middle Management			
First-Line Management			
Professionals/ Technical			
Clerical			
Shop Floor			
Union Leadership			

10
The Reward and Reinforcement System

With a thoroughly planned communication system and top-notch learning system, a change is destined to succeed. Or is it? A third critical change element, a reward and reinforcement system, needs to be integrated into the action plan. None of these systems exist in isolation. Each is closely tied to the other two. Every learning contact is an opportunity to communicate what has to change and why. Every communication that addresses the future state is part of the target's education regarding what will be expected of him or her. Every message that informs targets of where they are in the delta is an opportunity to recognize their progress and reinforce their efforts.

While this integration seems obvious to serious students of change, the third system, rewards and reinforcements, is frequently neglected, indeed often forgotten, by change agents. Change management should be easy because it is common sense and logic. Jim McGrath, director of Quality Management at Moen Faucets, calls it "profound common sense," profound and difficult.

To make change happen, you can't just talk about it, and you can't just teach people a new way. You need to systematically implement a thoughtful and comprehensive reward and reinforcement system.

WHY THIS EMPHASIS?
We have seen how the current state exerts a powerful hold on the target. The familiarity, comfort, and security of the current state keeps even eager targets from leaving without a few backward glances.

Built into the current state are many elements that hold targets in place or make it difficult for them to leave. You examined in detail in Chapters 4 and 7 the reasons why individuals have difficulty changing. The current state continues because people are comfortable within it, they know how to succeed in it, it has worked for so many years, and people know how to get rewarded for operating within it.

Some past rewards are very positive. The company grew in size and profitability over those years. Products became better and better. People got promoted. They got bigger paychecks, bonuses, health plans, pensions, and even, if they were very lucky, better food in the cafeteria.

Sometimes people stay in a current state not because the rewards are so great but because the alternatives could be worse. The company may have few opportunities for growth, but at least it is close to home and the traffic isn't too bad. The manager may be a dictator, but he's still better than the last manager.

Another critical element that holds the target in the present state is the company culture. Embedded into every company, department, location, and work group is a set of behaviors that over time have been identified as "the way things are done around here." Some behaviors are described in the employee handbook and job procedures. Some may be identified as the operating principles that guide the company's beliefs and behaviors. Some are more subtle. They are the "real" way to be successful. In fact, some of the really successful behaviors may actually fly in the face of the employee handbook or the operating principles printed right under the mission statement.

These behaviors have become second nature to employees over time. They are the way things get done. In manufacturing, many unofficial beliefs drive the current state, have contributed to the company's past success, and therefore have become an intrinsic part of the reward system:

- Having fun at work means you are goofing off.
- Short-term goals always drive this business.
- Mistakes are a career-limiting move around here.
- The end of the month is the best time to ship product.
- If you need 20 build 30 just in case.
- Every department must protect its own interests.
- Monday's supervisor was Friday's operator.
- Production heroes get the jobs out the door.
- The bigger the batch, the lower the unit cost.
- The faster the machine, the more economical the product.
- If you disagree, you are viewed as subversive, toxic waste.

These beliefs become part of the company. People who behave in support of those beliefs get rewarded. People who challenged them get punished. People who do not give up these cultural beliefs are not about to change. The beliefs can hold back people's progress in the delta.

The Belief	The Behavior
• Having fun at work means you are goofing off.	• So don't be playful.
• Short-term goals always drive this business.	• So don't bother thinking five years into the future.
• Mistakes are a career-limiting move around here.	• So keep your head down and don't experiment.
• The end of the month is the best time to ship product.	• So schedule all the training in the first half of the month.
• If you need 20 build 30 just in case.	• So don't tell the change agents about that secret storage space you always use.
• Every department must protect its own interests.	• So let the manufacturing engineering group go through this change first.
• Monday's supervisor was Friday's operator.	• So assume they will all be like the ones before.
• Production heroes get the jobs out the door.	• So don't worry, it will happen.
• The bigger the batch, the lower the unit cost.	• So forget all this activity-based costing, it doesn't make sense.
• The faster the machine, the more economical the product.	• So get better machinery, don't form teams.
• If you disagree, you are viewed as subversive, toxic waste.	• So keep your mouth shut!

SHIFTING THE BALANCE

The effective change agent helps the target leave the current state and move through the delta by altering the target's reward system. What was positive about the current state loses positive reinforcement. What was negative about the future state must become *more* positive than the current state. In addition, the delta must be made as safe and comfortable as possible.

Today		
Present +	Delta −	Future State +/−

Figure 10.1
Today's Balance

Tomorrow		
Present −	Delta +/−	Future State +

Figure 10.2
Tomorrow's Balance

Change agents can shift that balance in two ways.

1. They can design a change management plan that immediately and dramatically shifts the reward system from the present to the future. "Tomorrow, show up looking like the future state or die!" People either go flying through the delta or they find themselves in incredible pain.
2. They can design a plan that moves people out of the current state at a steady pace because each day they find the present less and less rewarding and find the future state more and more attractive.

Each alternative has advantages and disadvantages. "Change or die" gets people moving fast. It requires little from the communication or learning system. The major driver of the change is the reward system. You get rewarded if you change and are punished if you choose not to change. There are times when this is the most expedient change strategy to use. When the building is on fire there is little time for elaborate discussion of what it would feel like to be outside in the cool breeze of the future state. It is certainly not the time to have a three-hour training class on how to cope with fires in burning buildings. Get out of the building or die!

The company that says, "This building is on fire! Let's move, people," finds that people *will* move. At least it will look as though they have moved. They will use the new system, reorganize the shop floor, and show up in the new department, but the only thing that has moved is their bodies. Their behaviors, orientation to their jobs, their beliefs, values, and skills will still operate from the current-state structure. Slowly, over the course of a few weeks or months, they begin to shape the future to look much like the past. They change the change rather than change themselves. Are they unusually resistant people? No, they are normal, everyday people ordered to change without the benefit of a structured plan for communication, learning, *and* rewards and reinforcements.

This does not mean that changes using change management systems are necessarily slow. It does mean there is more time spent up front on the planning and organizing.

Sometimes "change now or die!" is the right way to manage change, but the flames had better be spreading very rapidly through the building before you use that method. Also you need to understand that this is a very expensive change strategy. It will only buy you a few weeks, months, or years. Then you will have to go back and rework the change using the more structured change management model.

Rapid change is becoming the norm. Living in a constant delta with a future state that forms and reforms almost daily means that certain changes will surface as *Change-Now-and-Ask-Questions-Later* changes. However, if the company has implemented a strong change management strategy and has designed effective change management systems, even do or die changes *can* use communication, learning, and rewards and reinforcements. *Change Now* (because) and *Ask Questions Later* (but here's the basic skill training that will at least get us to first base, and here is how we will monitor and reinforce the milestones through the delta). If the systems have been effectively used in the past, the targets will trust that rewards will come later.

BUILDING THE STRATEGY
The Future

It starts with the future. The communication system is built around a description of where the target is going. The learning system uses the skills and behaviors required in the future as the framework for its designs. The reward and reinforcement system starts by determining what will be rewarded in the future. This is a key business strategy, showing the organization the link between their future actions and the results of those actions—success. If you know what you want and where you want to be, you need to tie the reward system to that future. That is the carrot, the incentive or pull.

This means that the future state must have both measurable business objectives and measurable and observable people objectives. In Chapter 2 you saw the need to build a concrete picture of the future so that people could see themselves within it—how they would operate, use tools, and behave. Now you can take that concrete picture and tie a reward system to it. When you operate in the new way—use those new tools, skills, and behaviors—you will be rewarded. They might be the same measurements the company has always used, but with higher performance criteria. They may be entirely new measurements.

The Past

Simultaneously the measurements and standards that triggered rewards in the current state begin to dissolve. They go away, replaced by the new measurements and standards. If the other two systems, communication and learning, are working well, people can see this happening and understand why it is happening. They will be given opportunities to build the skills and incorporate the behaviors that enable them to achieve the new measurements and standards.

Remember that a key part of the current state is the behaviors and beliefs that have become embedded in the company and make up the unofficial definition of success within the culture.

It does no good to define the future state as a smooth flow of production across time if people who lie back for the first 20 days of the month and then go full steam ahead for the last 10 get the same reward as those who follow the new system.

Logic may show the need to increase inventory turns. People may be able to see how the cost of inventory is eating up the profitability of the company. However, if there has always been great comfort and security in seeing finished goods pile up in the warehouse and there is no better reward for those who increase turns than for those who stockpile, common sense seems to fly out the window and inventory builds.

Management and workers may go through a training class on team work and perform in exemplary fashion. However, if the foreman who has always kicked butt and taken names continues that behavior out on the floor and gets the same raise and support as the foreman trying out the new "coaching" behaviors, he will probably keep up that old behavior. The other foreman, seeing that the rewards are the same, may stop trying new behaviors that require extra effort and return to the old way as well.

The Delta

As they give up the old criteria of success and move to the new, targets sometimes take giant strides. They leap across the delta quickly, covering great chasms with a single bound. Sometimes they take baby steps so small you can go for weeks and not even see the movement across the delta. Slow or fast, movement toward the future state needs to be identified, measured, and reinforced. Old behaviors die hard. After all, they had years in which to become embedded. Even with the best of intentions, people who try to emulate new behavior will fall back on old ways. The reinforcement strategy is designed to recognize their effort to move forward, reward those efforts as well as the results, and make the new way so desirable that people work hard to sustain the new and not let themselves slip back.

Controlling cholesterol is a national pastime in the United States. Countless hours of lunch-room conversations are taken up comparing cholesterol counts and discussing the newest medical findings regarding ways to reduce cholesterol without having to control diet. This is because people hope the future state, a low cholesterol count, can be achieved without the pain of going through the delta, forgoing cheese, eggs, and red meat. All those lunch-time worriers have something in common. They leave the doctor's office after getting the bad news totally committed to lowering the count by watching what they eat. They are religious about their diets— for about two weeks.

Then one night, just before bed, they slip back into the old ways and have big plates of cheese and crackers. Suddenly it's all over. The diets are ruined. So the next day they have bacon at breakfast and butter and sour cream on their potatoes at lunch. One little slip in the delta and they see themselves back in the current state. They may or may not start over. This isn't logical.

One plate of cheese does not mean they can't change. It means they stumbled in the delta. If they could have seen progress in the weeks since the doctor visit and seen that the plate of cheese did not undo all the work done to date, just created a little blip in the progress chart, they would be more inclined to wake up the next morning and keep going on the diet. However, because the delta is not very pleasant, they use that "mistake" to scurry back to the current state. This entitles them to add a whole new repertoire to their lunch conversations about how hard they tried, how difficult it is to change—and it increases desire for a magic pill.

MAKING IT HAPPEN

The first step in designing a reward and reinforcement system is identifying what needs to be rewarded. The previous discussion has raised the issues to be examined. Using the future state picture of the *structures, processes, people,* and *culture,* the change agents can design business-level performance objectives that will be rewarded.

The learning system implementation will help you identify the behaviors and skills to be rewarded. The overall action plan or project plan helps you identify key milestones in the delta that will be measured and rewarded.

Reward The Future State

For many years there was a management myth that said workers only work for money; the only thing that motivated them was dollars in their paycheck. Research and results have debunked that myth. Workers work for money and a lot of other things as well. So one of the first issues in the design of a reward and reinforcement system is the rewards themselves.

Money is a reward. People should get paid for what they do. That pay should be fair and equitable and tied to the important behaviors and results that make the company successful. There are outstanding examples of companies designing innovative ways to do just that: gain sharing, profit sharing, skill-based pay, pay for knowledge, pay for improvement, and team-based pay are some systems being used.

Selecting the right financial reward system is a difficult process. There are many issues: individual versus team versus organizational incentives; the potential of pitting one operation or group against another; and potentially conflicting choices such as overtime pay versus pay for increasing inventory turns or on-time delivery versus quality improvement.

The best way for the change agents to educate themselves on the choices is to study companies that have already experimented and succeeded. An excellent place to find those companies is through the Association for Manufacturing Excellence. AME is an outstanding organization made up of manufacturing companies willing to experiment and serious about making change happen. Many AME members, who have been installing new compensation systems, have invited the membership in to see what they have done and contemplate how these various approaches would work for them.

Do not focus exclusively on the monetary reward system! There are myriad reasons why people get up and go to work each day, and only one of those is money. The type of work, working conditions, people they work with, autonomy or structure of the job, opportunities to learn and grow, and flexibility of their schedule are a few items people find rewarding in their work.

The more the change agents understand about what makes people feel good, the better they will be able to design those elements into the future state as rewards and reinforcements for changing.

Remember Dave at *Continental Can* who cried as he described the response of management when he shut down the line? He was getting rewarded for a behavior he thought was right. It was a behavior that in the past had gotten him in trouble.

> Being valued and treated as a the owner of the operation is an incredible reward for Dave. It made him cry. How many people cry when they talk about a raise they got?

> Remember Burt Hoefs at *Gates Rubber Company* in Arkansas? Burt was a great sponsor of change. Out on the shop floor in one of the cells making automotive belts, there is a letter. It is covered in plastic and pasted to the side of one of the machines. It is a letter from a customer addressed directly to the people in that cell. The letter thanks them for solving a major problem the customer had, working so fast and directly with the customer, and being such great people with whom to do business. That letter has a place of honor in that work cell. If you go wandering around in the shop and stop at that cell to talk with those people, it is inevitable that they will show you that letter. When they do, they trail their fingers over it with reverence. It is a reward. It is a key part of the reason those people get up each day and come to work to make automotive belts.

Move Through the Delta

Because it is so easy to stay in the current state and so hard to live in the delta, change agents need to make the delta a more comfortable place. A good project plan that recognizes incremental steps through the delta is also a reinforcement plan; it tells the change agents to watch for certain behaviors, measurements, and changes. When they occur, the targets should get rewarded for the progress they have made. This is a vital step in the change management process. It cannot be left to chance. Missing the celebration of key milestones, tacking a reward on too late or missing some of the people who progressed—these actions send a message to the targets telling them how serious the company is about making this change successful.

The first rule of the reward and reinforcement system in the delta is: reinforce the milestones. There is a second, equally important rule: *forget doughnuts and pizza!* They have been done to death. They have been done very poorly, showing up without being linked to an actual, measurable, identifiable milestone, given to the wrong people, brought in three weeks after the milestone, being the only recognition used, and used, and used! Change agents must be creative in designing innovative ways to let people know that milestones have been achieved and that the people involved are valued for their contributions. Some examples of innovative recognition are:

• Name a sandwich in the cafeteria for the team or individual to be recognized.

- Send a box of candy or a gift certificate for a video rental to their home.
- Have the president of the company broadcast a thank-you message on e-mail or voice mail telling employees what this person or group accomplished and what it means to the company.

For years, Tom Peters has been highlighting companies that are creative and innovate in rewarding employees. There are myriad examples in fast-changing companies today. Get creative, get serious, get to work.

There is a third rule regarding the reinforcers used to help people through the delta. Change the reinforcers often. Even pizza and doughnuts had value once, but they were used too often. A rich variety of reinforcement techniques sends a strong message that the change agents are very serious about monitoring and managing the delta. That tells the targets a lot about how serious this change effort is and helps them decide whether or not they will choose to change.

The Sponsor's Role

It would appear in this discussion that all the work is done by the change agents. That is not true. The change agents are responsible for planning this key system of the change process. However, the majority of the rewards should come not from the change agents but from the sponsors. They are critical in the implementation of the reward and reinforcement system. Performance accountability, whether in a hierarchical or a matrix organization, is implemented between the employee and his or her management. Therefore management plays a key role in the changing performance accountability and the accompanying changes in the reward system.

Chapter 5 identified this involvement as a key role of the sponsors. This key role becomes an action item in the design of the reward and reinforcement system. This is where sponsors see what they have to do, when they have to do it, with whom, and using what vehicles. This is one of those key places where the partnership between sponsors and change agents will make or break a change effort.

II. REAL WORLD   *Treetop Manufacturing Company*

CHARLIE

They had worked so hard for so many months, but it looked like they had blown it! All the careful planning, the hours and hours spent on defining where they wanted to go and how to get there, and now it seemed like it was all unravelling.

Charlie and his team were once more sitting around at the end of a very long day. How many of these late-night meetings had they had over the past year? Charlie looked at his team. They were tired, dispirited, and worn out. Everything had seemed to be going so well. They had done a good job designing a communication plan. They integrated it with the 100 Percent Solution team's messages, and the feedback from workers and management was acceptance of the need to change and a lot of excitement about the kind of changes engineering would go through.

As they rolled out the education and training, that enthusiasm had continued. People were learning how to work together. They accepted the new tools, CAD system, QFD model, involvement of sales and customers, and closer relationship with the people in manufacturing. In fact, in many instances, the targets were grabbing the changes and taking them further than Charlie and his team ever thought they would. The future state was changing and getting better and better as the targets became their own change agents.

Over the past few weeks, however, all that momentum seemed to slow down. Then, last week, it came to a screeching halt. Last Tuesday was the day the new reorganization of the department was announced. New job descriptions and performance standards were unveiled. A whole management layer was taken out of the operation, and many of the people who had been in the department were now assigned out in the manufacturing operation. Some people were assigned as permanent members of cross-functional teams, others as part-time. None of this was a surprise to people. Charlie and his team had been laying the groundwork for these changes for a long time. People didn't seem opposed to the idea. Most people were not even unhappy about their assignments. Everything should have gone smoothly.

The questions started immediately after people got their assignments and the information about their new jobs. Charlie and his team did not have the answers.

- Will I still get paid the same?
- How about additional pay for the new skills I've learned?
- Is my performance review going to be affected by what those guys in manufacturing do?
- How on earth do you expect to measure me on teamwork?
- Will my seniority be affected by this move?
- What is the career path in this new position?
- Who is my manager, now, Charlie or Keith?

As Charlie's group struggled to answer these questions a groundswell of fear and anger seemed to grow. It spread through the whole department, and today Ken Willinger handed Charlie a letter signed by every single person in the department except those on the Change Team.

To: Charlie Kellerman

From: Everyone

Re: THE CHANGES

We know we have to change. We understand that you, Tom, Jane, and Sam have worked long and hard to make these changes, but we need you to know that the changes you announced this week are very disruptive to each of us and to the department. We were willing to go along with them because we understood the logic behind them. Most of us feel we are ready for the changes. We have had a lot of training and are ready to try out our new skills.

However, there is a very serious problem with these changes You and your team are playing with our livelihood. You changed our reporting relationships, redefined our jobs and the way in which we are measured and compensated, but you can't answer some simple questions about how those changes affect us. This makes us very nervous.

We respectfully ask that you put these changes on hold until and unless you can give us the answers to the questions about how and by whom we will be judged, and how we will be compensated in the new structure.

While the team's first reaction to the memo had been anger, that feeling had quickly died. As they sat around talking they each recognized that they understood where everyone in the department was coming from. Those people were right to raise these issues.

"That memo shows we have already changed a lot around here," said Tom. "We've encouraged them to take more ownership and to be greater stakeholders in what occurs. Well, that's just what they did. Two or three years ago they would have gone like sheep to the new reporting relationship, and we would never have heard about their fears and concerns. This memo is great. They are telling us that as change agents we made a mistake. We forgot to address a whole area of the change process that is critical to them. So let's do it. They are not saying they won't change. They are saying they want more information about how this change will affect them."

"Okay, Tom," Jane sighed. "I guess you're right. I've been thinking about those same things myself ever since we began to put the new structure together. It's funny. I didn't really think about it from the perspective of others. I was thinking about myself. If I'm going to transfer to work under Joan Schwartz at the Lexington plant for 50 percent of my time for the next couple of years I wondered what that would do to my seniority and to my pay, but we've been so busy with all the ongoing changes, I just let that go. I'd like some answers myself."

Charlie didn't say anything, but he was remembering a night months ago when he and his wife went out to dinner and Charlie had begun to understand his own fears and resistance. One of the things that had been worrying him for a long time was whether he could do the job of managing this "Future State" department and what it would mean for his career. How could he have missed this whole area for the department when it was so important to him?

"Well, let's get some answers, Jane." Charlie reached for the phone and called Sandra Jimnitz from human resources. "Sandy, we need some help down here. Could you come and talk with us?"

When Charlie hung up the phone he turned back to the team and said, "Now, in the meantime, how do we respond to this memo?"

SARAH

Engineering had done Sarah a huge favor. When Charlie told her about the memo from his people Sarah turned pale. The 100 Percent team had not done much better than Charlie in this area, and they were just about to announce major reorganizations of the groups. In addition, at three of the plants the plant managers were starting to formalize the cell structures on several lines.

Sarah's team, like Charlie's, began to work on this issue with fierce attention. As engineering did, they saw that things had already moved far into the future, and instead of arbitrarily designing performance systems and compensation plans, they formed a task force made up of the people affected by the changes. They sent them out to find models of effective measurement and reward systems and charged them to recommend the way they should work at Treetop. The task force was highly visible, and its work was known throughout the company. Meanwhile, people were willing to bet on the future and on the fact that these issues would be worked out. They agreed to change, move into new functions, and work under new job descriptions with the understanding that this was the delta and things still needed to be worked out. Even engineering, much to Charlie and his groups' satisfaction, recalled their memo and went to work.

This whole issue had another benefit. It made Sarah and her team think a lot about rewards and recognition. They realized that they had not only failed to build the reward system needed to support the future state; they had paid little attention to the need to reward people as they moved *to* the future state.

"There's a tremendous amount of change going on out there," Sarah commented. "It's draining our resources and our energy, both as a company and as individuals. We have to get product out the door and to build new business, products, and customers, and in the midst of that we are making major changes. People are learning new skills, struggling with new behaviors, trying out new systems and tools, and working with different people. It's as if we have turned this whole company upside down.

"People get tired. They get confused. They can't always tell if they are doing things right. We need to give them some energy, clarity, and feedback. We also need to help them lighten up a little. Everyone around here looks so grim. Nobody is having much fun."

Within two weeks Sarah's team had addressed these issues. In the cafeteria in each plant and office, a huge wall chart went up one Wednesday morning. It showed in cartoons and pictures the "old" Treetop on the left and the "new" Treetop on the extreme right. In the middle, in the delta, there were cartoon depictions of the various ongoing changes. Cartoon people danced through the delta, some falling down, some racing across the void, some looking frightened, and some looking excited. At the bottom of the chart, tracking across the delta, was a timeline with key milestones identified: the announcement of the changes, installation of the new order entry system, the first cell operation at the Lexington plant.

Over the next few weeks, the workers saw something new at Treetop. Management began to talk more about the victories in the delta: at a company-wide level, department levels, and individual levels. People who had changed heard from management.

- John Shane began to show up unexpectedly all over the company, walking up to people who had done a good job of changing, shaking their hands and thanking them.
- One Friday, the South Bend plant announced it was shutting down an hour early. Everyone was invited out into the parking lot where a tent had been set up with ice-cream sundaes, a band, and banners. The management group put on a series of silly skits representing "their" fears and concerns as the changes had occurred.
- As people finished training classes, went back to work, and tried out the new tools, skills, and behaviors, they found unexpected and unusual validation that Treetop knew what they were doing and appreciated it.

   A gift certificate to a great local restaurant.

   A Friday afternoon off with pay.

   A sandwich named for them in the cafeteria.

   A chocolate bar with the word "Thanks" left at their work station.

   A personal note from John Shane tucked into their paycheck envelope.

The work involved in sending these messages of appreciation and recognition was incredible. Sarah thought her people were maxed out before they got to this recognition thing, but this really taxed them. She noticed something exciting, however. It also energized them. They loved thinking up new ways to let people know they were moving through the delta and were appreciated for it.

She decided she needed to let them know how much *they* were appreciated and recognized. "I'm going to have a hard time being as clever and creative in rewarding them as they have been with everyone else," she thought.

III. TOOLS FOR CHANGE

THE REWARD AND REINFORCEMENT PLAN

To set up an effective reward and reinforcement system, you can use a simple chart that will give you a framework for planning.

The Present	The Delta	The Future
• What is currently rewarded? Skills	• What are the milestones in this change? Project related	• What will be rewarded? Skills
Behaviors	People related	Behaviors
• Which of those skills and behaviors are formally identified; which are informal? Formal	• How will these milestones be measured?	• How will those skills and behaviors be identified and rewarded? Formally
Informal	• How will these milestones be celebrated?	Informally
• What are the rewards? Formal		• What will be the rewards? Formal
Informal		Informal

As the answers to these questions develop, define the roles of the sponsors and change agents.

Reward and Reinforcement Assignments

The Present	The Delta	The Future
Sponsor Activities	Sponsor Activities	Sponsor Activities
Change Agent Activities	Change Agent Activities	Change Agent Activities

PART FOUR

Putting It All Together

A constant state of change becomes the norm. While there have been periods of great upheaval and change throughout history, in civilization and in your company, these periods of upheaval were usually followed by a long period of stability and calm. People had time to adjust to the "new way" and in many instances it became the "present state" for years and years.

That is not the case today. Every indication is that it will not be that way for a long time, if ever again. Technology has linked people together and pulls them forward. The whole world has shrunk and is accessible to us with a keystroke or a dial tone.

The ability to live comfortably in the delta—a place that is unstable and constantly changing—is what will separate successful and unsuccessful companies, what will separate employees who like to go to work from those who cannot stand the tension and the stress.

That delta does *not* have to be a place of pain. Solid change management principles can guide the company and the employees through that delta. However, very few companies practice those principles in a structured, organized way. If the delta is to become a manageable constant, companies will have to change the way they manage change. This book has laid out the logic behind the change process and presented three tools to help people survive in the delta.

It is not enough, however, to read this book and nod in agreement. Development of strong sponsors and the application of those tools—the communication, learning, and reward and reinforcement system—requires planning, discipline, and resources. For most companies this will be a change in the way they change.

Three change agents from a medium-sized manufacturing company attended a change management workshop last year. They were the primary change agents, responsible for implementing a major restructuring of the company's manufacturing operations. At the end of the two days they were inspired. They had been doing a lot of the things discussed, but recognized that there was much more to be done. They went back to the office the next day and asked for a meeting with the president, their primary sponsor. They explained what they learned that week, what they were already doing, and what needed to be done to manage the change process itself.

He listened carefully and nodded in agreement at every point they made. Their closing remarks included a recommendation for laying out a strategy for change management. They wanted to bring in some outside resources to help them design the change systems, assess the skills and knowledge of the sponsors and other change agents, and help understand the degree and type of resistance throughout the company. The president agreed. The three went home that Friday night feeling rejuvenated. They had greater knowledge, tools to work with, and the promise of outside resources to help them. That was Friday.

On Monday, the president called them into his office. "Before you go running off hiring consultants and spending money, I want you to know I have been doing a lot of thinking about what you said last week. I agree with everything you said. We have got to manage this change process better, but I'm not as sure as I was last week that we have to go to such elaborate lengths to do it. Basically, everything you laid out last week is common sense. We have a lot of smart people around here. This hasn't been that good a year and I can't throw more money at this change. Look, all you have to do is let people know you are serious about making this change work. You don't need all that assessment and detailed planning you guys were talking about last week. I've written a memo. I want you to read it before I send it out. It will go to everyone who is in a management position. I know you need their help with these changes. So I've told them in the memo the importance of managing change and that I personally will hold them responsible for making sure the changes are managed well. This will get the message across to our people. This will get you the change management you need. They will do it because I told them to."

The team is still struggling. So is the management cascade. So is the president. He can't understand why they don't just "do" it.

Yes, it is common sense, but a key part of the common sense of change management is that it must be planned, organized, and applied in a structured, systematic way to help people live in the delta and move toward the future state.

The changes themselves drain resources from the ongoing business of the company and from the quarterly profitability. It *is* hard to assign more resources to assessment and planning, but the choice not to do so is a perilous choice.

In Part 1 the change process was described as a puzzle, with individual pieces making up the whole. Throughout this book you have examined those individual pieces. Now it is time to put them all together.

Here in Part 4 you will pull together the application issues previously discussed and lay out an implementation plan to help turn good intentions into a plan of action.

11
A Strategy for Change Implementation

There are three major steps in the change management process.

1. Define the future.
2. Assess the present in relation to that desired future.
3. Help people through the delta.

One key element will make all this happen: an implementation plan.

Without that plan the best companies will do a lot of the things discussed in this book. The problem is they probably won't do them all. The tools and techniques will be applied haphazardly, dependent on the intuitive skills of the change agents and their ability to teach what they don't understand.

Who makes this implementation plan? The change agents. It is a key part of their job. How do they do it? That's what this chapter is all about.

STRATEGY, PLANNING, AND RESOURCE REQUIREMENTS

Good planning starts with a strategy. That strategy leads to the actual planning process. The strategy must step up to the issue that the planning process itself requires resources: time, dollars, consultants, training, and personnel. The plan will identify the resource requirements for the actual changes as well.

179

A CHANGE MANAGEMENT STRATEGY

Whether you are contemplating a change or are already three years into it, now is the time to lay out a strategy for planning the change. It is never too late. Even if you have been thrashing around in a delta for eight months, you can still get a hold of the change process itself, set some parameters around that process, and help people move through the delta.

What Is a Change Management Planning Strategy?

- It is a commitment on the part of the key change agents to plan the people side of the change.
- It is the agreement by the key sponsors that this planning is a major part of the change and that they will support it.
- It is the coming together of those change agents prepared to lay out the steps, time frames, and resource requirements.
- It is the integration of all the important elements of change management applied against the three key steps in the process:

The Change Implementation Plan

	Define the Future	Assess the Current State	Manage the Delta
Information Gathering			
Resource Requirements			
Change Agent Responsible			

THE PLANNING PROCESS
Define the Future

If change starts with a need to be something other than what you are, you must be open to the forces, current and anticipated, that create instability in the current state. Today's best companies work hard to ensure that they are open to those forces and that they seek them out. The discomfort from those forces drives the company and its workforce to ask hard questions about what *could* be.

Using the key elements of *process, structure, people,* and *culture,* the company can then build a common, integrated picture of where it is going. While that picture is, and should be, open to constant evaluation and revision, the change agents can identify the resource requirements and assign responsibility for change.

Process, structure, people, and *culture* are the framework for gathering data and answering the following questions. Identify the resource requirements and assign responsibility for each activity.

The Future

	Define the Future

Information Gathering	• Processes
	What processes are key to the company's vision?
	How will those processes operate?
	How will they be measured?
	How will they be determined to be working successfully?
	What will be firm and fixed through time?
	What will be subject to ongoing change?
	What will be the same as it is now?
	What will be different?
	
	• Structures
	How should the company be organized?
	What should be the relationship between the horizontal and vertical structures?
	How much management should there be?
	Where should that management be placed?
	
	• People
	What is the role of management?
	What is the relationship between departments?
	What is the role of the worker?
	What competencies will be required?
	    by management
	    by the workforce
	    by vendors
	    by customers
	
	• Culture
	How will people behave?
	What will they believe is important?
	What kind of rules will the organization have?

Resource Requirements	• Time: _____ • Dollars: _____ • Personnel: _____ • Consultants: _____ • Training: _____
Change Agent Responsible	• Primary Change Agents: _____ _____

Assess the Current State

Because the future state is being shaped out of those four key elements, they should be used as the framework for assessing the present.

The Present

	Assess the Current State

Information Gathering	• Processes
	How do those processes operate today?
	How are they measured?
	
	• Structures
	How is the company organized?
	What is the relationship between the horizontal and vertical structures?
	How much management is there?
	Where is that management placed?
	
	• People
	What is the role of management?
	What is the relationship between departments?
	What is the role of the worker?
	What competencies are required?
	   by management
	   by the workforce
	   by vendors
	   by customers
	
	• Culture
	How do people behave?
	What do they believe is important?
	What kind of rules does the organization have?

Resource Requirements	• Time: _____ • Dollars: _____ • Personnel: _____ • Consultants: _____ • Training: _____
Change Agent Responsible	• Primary Change Agents: _____ _____

Manage the Delta

Change management can help people be comfortable in the delta, not to fear it, and learn to use it for growth—their own and the company's.

Knowing the key variables that will affect what happens in the delta, the change agents need to gather data about the change and the change process. They need to find out:

- Who are the change sponsors?
- How willing are they to be effective sponsors?
- How able are they—how knowledgeable of the change process and the role of the sponsor?
- Are all the change agents identified?
- What is their willingness level? Their ability level?
- What targets will be affected?
- In what order?
- To what degree?
- What will be the targets' resistance issues?

The delta is not a narrow highwire, but a broad band of time and space. The targets, sponsors, and change agents can move forward, coalescing, reforming, experimenting, and changing in the delta. To succeed there, it is vital that the sponsors, with coaching from the change agents, set some boundaries around the delta:

- What changes are going on?
- What is their relationship to one another?
- What are the rules as the company changes?
    Everyone stays open and flexible.
    Change ideas come from everywhere.
    Management is careful not to hurt people.
    Everyone in the company owns the changes and the future.
    No changes are permanent.

Now the three systems of change management can be defined in order to move the company through the delta.

The Delta

	Manage the Delta
Information Gathering	• Identify and assess the key players
	• Set the delta boundaries
	• Design the change systems
	Communication System
	Learning System
	Reward and Reinforcement System

Resource Requirements	• Time: _____
	• Dollars: _____
	• Personnel: _____
	• Consultants: _____
	• Training: _____
Change Agent Responsible	• Primary Change Agents: _____
	_____

Lay Out the Plan

There are big changes, small changes, and huge changes going on in companies today. As companies get better at this change business they begin to form a picture of all the changes (see the fishbone diagram in Chapter 2). Big, small, huge, and minute fit into a picture of the overarching changes needed.

The exercise just presented—gathering the information to lay out a plan of action—needs to start with the overarching change at the most senior levels of the company. Simultaneously each primary change agent group needs to be doing this for their own change project. It would be smarter to do it sequentially, but there is no time. This makes the job of coordinating change efforts even more critical.

Coordination is a project management skill. Project management and the tools of project management clearly are a great asset to the change process. The discussion in this book affects only the human elements of the change process. The actual changes to be made in the processes, structures, people, and culture are not addressed here—they require further skills and resources to be acquired elsewhere.

Both the actual organizational change action steps and the people-related action steps need to be integrated using project management tools. There are excellent books, courses, and software tools available to provide support and guidance in the development of a total project management strategy.

THE PLANNING RESOURCES

Resource requirements are a key issue in laying out what has to change, when, and how. However, planning itself also absorbs resources. It is important to identify the requirements of planning and determine up front if there is sponsorship for the process.

The key question sponsors have to answer is whether they choose to make a commitment to managing the change. That decision should be pragmatic, based on an analysis of the cost of managing the change as opposed to not managing it.

The Cost of Change

What is the cost of managing these changes?

- Selecting and preparing change agents $_____
- Planning the change and the change management $_____
- Developing and sustaining strong sponsorship $_____
- Reducing resistance $_____
- Putting change systems in place $_____
  - Communication system
  - Learning system
  - Reward/reinforcement system

Total $_____

What is the cost of *not* managing these changes?

- In the Present $_____
  - Refusal to Change $_____
  - Sabotage $_____
- In the Delta $_____
  - Physical stress $_____
  - Emotional stress $_____
  - Replacement hiring $_____
  - Retraining $_____
  - Running dual systems $_____
  - Close supervision $_____
  - Lost productivity $_____
  - Time to implement $_____
- Organizational Impact
  - Loss of strong employees $_____
  - Extra effort on the next change $_____

Total $_____

CHARLIE

What a year this had been! Charlie reached for his gin and tonic and leaned back in the beach chair. Jamaica was great and far enough away from Treetop that Charlie had thought he could forget about the company, at least for a week. It was January and a snow storm was sweeping across the middle of the country. It was sunny, warm, and relaxing here, but Charlie couldn't stop thinking about Treetop.

"I worked so hard this past year to help put all those changes in place," he told his wife at breakfast, "I guess my mind is still in fifth gear. I decided this morning while I was walking on the beach that I'm not going to fight it. I am going to use this week of sitting and soaking up sun to think through what I have done this past year and what is coming up for me."

That is what he had been doing all day. The luxury of just sitting and thinking had sent his mind reeling at first. A jumble of images swept in: Ken Willinger's face when they announced the changes; his team, tired and worn down so many late nights; John Shane at the general meeting fielding questions; John Shane and Keith working out Keith's issues; the conference room filled with charts of information and diagrams; the sad, sad feeling on Joe Schneider's last day, when he chose to retire rather than to change.

"What did we do right?" Charlie asked himself. "Were there some things we could have done better? We certainly thought a lot about the future, but while we carefully designed how it would look, we kept ourselves open to modifying and adjusting it as we went along. That was the key to our success. We set out toward a destination, but we kept ourselves loose and flexible along the way."

Charlie thought about Sarah and the 100 Percent Team. If there was one thing that they really had done right, it was hooking up with Sarah. The changes Sarah was charged to make would not have been possible if she and Charlie had been in conflict. His changes *had* to fit into what she was doing or they would have all spent this past year fighting instead of building a future state together. John Shane had not seen that, but the change agents had. That was OK. Charlie had come to understand that those kinds of integrating insights were part of the change agent's job.

What John *had* done was become a good sponsor. He really did not have any idea what he had asked of Charlie, Sarah, and the company when he launched all this change, but as the future began to define itself he had not flinched. He had looked at it and said, "Let's go!"

Charlie's team had been outstanding. He remembered when they first started to meet, how reluctant the team was to embrace some of the ideas of what engineering could look like. Partnering with people from the plants, sales, marketing, and customers had seemed like just a pipe dream. But today, just 12 months later, it was hard to imagine things had ever been any other way. Just before he left Charlie had done a performance review with Tom. The new performance objectives were not going to be a problem for Tom. Working in cooperation with marketing to develop a major modification on two of the household appliance lines was coming along very well. Tom used to be a real loner. He had bad-mouthed the plant operation every chance he got and was even worse in his assessment of the salespeople, but at his review he didn't want to talk about what he had accomplished this year. At the edge of his chair, he leaned forward and began to describe to Charlie what he thought they could accomplish *next* year as he worked *with* the plant and sales. Charlie restrained himself from smiling too broadly. This was great!

There were still problems. His department, a lot smaller now that so many engineers were assigned directly to the plants or to project teams, was struggling to support the remote locations with the right drawings and information. The new CAD system was great, but Charlie noticed that while the younger people seemed to get it right away, some of the older engineers were not using it to its maximum. "That's okay," Charlie thought. "That will come in time."

One problem had really surprised him. The two secretaries and the clerk responsible for the drawings seemed really depressed. Their jobs had changed somewhat, but it had not been a wrenching, dramatic change for them. Charlie couldn't figure it out. They were hardly affected. What was the matter with them, moping around all the time?

Then one day it occurred to him that he had not heard Heather's voice much all day. Heather sat just outside his office, and he had always enjoyed the sound of her cheerful voice greeting people as they walked around the department, checking on how they felt that day, whether their kids were OK, and what she could do to help them out.

Now there weren't so many people to talk to any more. Heather's formal job duties had not changed, but her unofficial job of department morale officer had been cut in half. She missed all the people who used to stop by her desk each day. She missed that part of her job.

Change came at you from unexpected sources. If there was one thing Charlie had learned this year, it was that no one could anticipate the effects of all this change. Better to assume that there were lots of surprises in store and keep your eyes open for them.

Charlie ordered another gin and tonic and thought about himself. He had been a sponsor, a change agent, and a target for the past 12 months. How had he done?

As a sponsor he was pretty satisfied. He understood the depth and implications of the changes that were being made in engineering, and he had fought hard to get all the resources he could to support the changes. He struggled to be available to communicate with his people and to encourage and support them. He had stepped up to hard issues, negotiated with other departments, and gone to John several times for clarification and support.

He was pretty satisfied with his job as change agent. He had learned a lot this year about what that job was all about. It was tough, but satisfying too. Gradually, over the year, he had seen the reorganization take hold. He watched the new tools become a part of the way engineering was done in Treetop. He saw a change in the way engineering was viewed in the company. Engineers were no longer seen as prima donnas. They were a part of the team. He had made that happen, and he was proud of what he had done to get them through the delta.

It was as a target of change that Charlie was still feeling uneasy. He wasn't sure if he liked being the manager of a department that was so lean. He was having trouble managing people who were suddenly feeling so empowered. People, including even the secretaries, were taking the initiative to raise issues, contact people from other departments, solve problems and tell him about it later; all the things he had worked so hard to put in place—but he kept forgetting that.

He had to keep biting his tongue not to challenge their right to do these things. He kept wanting to jump in and tell them what to do when they were struggling with a problem. He got really scared when some of them took the initiative, but did things differently from the way he would have done them. What if they screwed up? What if they did it wrong? How was Charlie supposed to know when to stop them and when to let them go? Somehow he had always known how to do this with the change team, but he was not very good at it yet with the day-to-day work.

Over the past few weeks Charlie had noticed something else about himself. He was getting bored. This had been an exciting and challenging year for him. He had learned a lot and done a lot. Maybe his real job was not managing a department but changing a department. It seemed he was pretty good at it. Treetop was on its way to the future. Charlie wondered if he should stay with Treetop or find another company that needed a skilled change agent and lots of change.

That was enough thinking for today. Charlie turned to his wife in the beach chair next to him. "Race you to the water, Susan," he said, and jumped out of his chair.

SARAH

There was not a grain of sand or a wave in sight, just miles and miles of open space anchored by snow-covered peaks. Sarah was hiding and resting, just like Charlie. She and her family had nestled into a cabin in the mountains to get reacquainted. Sarah hadn't been around much over the past year. Her family had been incredibly patient. They understood what she was trying to do at Treetop and had given her lots of support. That had made it easier, but Sarah was determined to take full advantage of this quiet week to be with them 100 percent.

"There it was again," she thought, "100 percent." She couldn't seem to stop thinking in Treetop change terms. So today, before anyone else woke up, she put on her hiking boots, grabbed a walking stick, and headed up to the plateau they had discovered yesterday. Here, for a few hours she could enjoy the solitude and think about the past year. Like Charlie, she needed to sort out what had happened and how she felt about it.

She felt good. Good things were happening at Treetop and she had helped make them happen. Marketing had done a customer survey last week and the results made the whole company smile. On-time deliveries had soared. Orders were being shipped complete, schedules were being met. Susan Sullivan, the CFO, had called her just before she left.

"I thought you might like to leave on a high note, Sarah. The profitability numbers for last quarter increased by 15 percent. The increases seemed to come from reduced inventory carrying costs and faster turnaround on receivables. Our head count has gone down too, though we've been able to do that entirely by voluntary retirements and not replacing people in jobs that have been eliminated."

Yesterday she had received a fax from Keith Bailer, who had found her in her mountain hideaway, with the production numbers for last week. He had scrawled a note at the bottom. "Sarah, note the rework numbers, almost zero! You were right. We *can* build quality in!"

Sarah didn't think she would ever throw that note away. Maybe she would frame it. She had helped make change happen at Treetop. At least she had started the process. Over the past few months the change efforts seemed to be taking on a life of their own. Her team tried to keep track of the major change initiatives on the fishbone in the War Room, but they couldn't keep up any more. In departments and across department boundaries people were asking "what if we . . . ?" The momentum was building and change was becoming a way of life around Treetop.

How had all this happened? What had Sarah and her team done? Was there some way to boil the whole year's effort into a simple formula or blueprint? With so many changes taking off, she began to think that her most important job now was not to make change happen but to *help* change happen by teaching other change agents what she and her team had done.

Maybe there was a blueprint. The 100 Percent Team had used a structured reengineering methodology that was well documented. They had kept careful notes and designed a procedure manual to help change agents in the departments. They also imported an excellent project management methodology and were rigorous in using its tools to track and monitor the change efforts.

However, deciding what to change and integrating the changes in a project path was the easy part. Getting people to change was the real work, the work of which Sarah was most proud. What had they done that had worked so well?

"It takes people to get people to change," Sarah thought. From John Shane to Chester Knudson, the night foreman at Lexington, the sponsorship for the changes had been carefully developed. The team had left nothing to chance. They had taught the management how to sponsor and then made sure they were plugged into the sponsor activities their targets needed from them. That was the toughest part of this "people stuff." The management of Treetop was a good group, but they were all targets as well as sponsors. Sarah remembered that long, hard meeting between John Shane and Keith Bailer. Supporting the sponsors, stroking them, coaching them, being patient with them, understanding them—what a job!

In addition to the sponsors, the team had paid careful attention to the change agents scattered around the company. They had all attended workshops to understand the change process and to learn how to use the change systems. Sarah's group had fought hard to make sure that those change agents had the sponsorship they needed out in the trenches. They brought all the change agents together periodically to coach them and give them a chance to learn from one another.

Working with the targets had been the most satisfying part of this whole project for Sarah and the team. Helping them face their change-related issues and decide to give change a chance felt really good. As they began to hit the milestones in the delta, the team had had great fun coming up with clever ways to celebrate and recognize them for what they had done. They took pride and satisfaction from watching the targets move into the future.

Her team was great. Sarah had been careful to watch that they did not get burned out throughout the year. That was not easy. She had watched for signs of stress and overwork, and as things were about to come to a boiling point she would shut everything down for a few hours and take everyone to a baseball game or out for a long, long lunch. The team's families had suffered through this year, too. Several times the team had hosted their families for an evening dinner in the conference room they used, filled with their charts and plans. Even the children seemed to get a better understanding of what their absent parents were up to.

From watching other companies the team had learned that an important issue was the need to have their "special project" work included with their regular objectives. Sarah talked to John Shane about this and he informed the management team that if they had anyone on the change projects they were to consider that at review time.

Her team had all received good merit increases this year and nice bonuses. They had learned and grown over the year, too. In their plans for next year was an invitation to other companies across the country who were interested in making similar changes to come to Treetop and see what they had done and how they had done it. Two team members were writing an article for an industry magazine explaining Treetop's changes and change process. Sarah had watched these people develop new skills and had seen the pride and satisfaction they had taken in their accomplishments. While she had worried all year about making sure they got the rewards and recognition they needed and deserved, by the end of the year they were taking care of that themselves.

There had been some sad times too. Joe Schneider, the plant manager at South Bend, couldn't make it. He fought the changes with every fiber of his body. John Shane had first asked Sarah to work around Joe and protect him, but in the end that could not be done. Joe had kept blocking her team and the other change agents and had pushed hard against Keith and even John, trying to get them to give up on these "crazy ideas." Sarah, Charlie, and Keith had spent many hours trying to resolve this problem, and finally they had gone to John Shane to tell him Keith would offer Joe an early retirement package. The whole company was sad to see Joe go, but they didn't let him slink away in defeat. He was honored and thanked for all the things he had done. Joe had been angry for months. You could see how it had been eating at him. During his final week, however, through the dinners and lunches and as cards and faxes of good wishes filled his in-basket, he had begun to change.

"I still think you people are crazy," he growled at one luncheon. "It's encouraging to hear you talk about what us 'old timers' have done, though. At least you aren't going to throw everything away. Who knows, maybe you are right to do what you are doing. I wish you a lot of luck."

Sponsors, change agents, and targets: help them to understand their roles and give them the tools and you've got a change. Those tools proved to be very effective. The team used the three systems of change very effectively. They had not let communication, learning, or rewards happen haphazardly. It had been a tremendous amount of work to put those systems in place. Often Sarah and the team had been frustrated and attempted to short circuit the system. "We've done so much, why aren't the sponsors taking more responsibility for writing their own speeches and figuring out who needs to hear what, when? Aren't they ever going to learn?"

Some had learned. There were examples of great initiatives in each of the systems, but the overall responsibility had always stayed with the change teams.

That, too, was changing. In the past few weeks, Sarah had noticed that managers all over the company were supporting change efforts with words *and* actions without a lot of prompting. The training department became a major resource for many areas where change was occurring. The human resources department was investigating all kinds of new compensation systems. Treetop was turning into a great place to work.

As the sun started to heat up the rocks Sarah was sitting on, she turned her thoughts to the future. What was next for her? She and her team had become such a strong change agent force, she hated to see them break up. Yet it seemed as if their work was over. That is, until last week when John Shane called her into his office again.

"Sarah, you know we have always had an interest in the Lulif Company in Dallas. They have been a major competitor of ours for years and a real thorn in our side. Remember when you did that study on them a few years ago? We figured that the best thing we could do was to buy them and make them a key part of our business instead of our major competitor. We backed off for a lot of reasons, but I remember that one of the key ones was that they were so different from us in the way they did business and in the way they ran their company that it would be too hard to integrate them into Treetop. Well, I've been thinking about that a lot lately. Their president called me last week and said they would entertain an offer from us. I've been thinking that we should make that offer. We are in a great cash position and, even more important, we now have the skills, tools, and experts to manage the changes in Lulif so that it could become a part of Treetop. What do you think?"

"Another major change project," thought Sarah. "This one even more difficult than changing Treetop. Lulif's culture, its management style, its market philosophy were almost totally opposite Treetop's."

"John, it's a great opportunity," Sarah said out loud. "Let's do it. With one clear understanding first. You have a first-rate, expert change agent group in Treetop that can make this work. However, Lulif won't do all the changing. Treetop is going to be in for even more changes as Lulif comes on board."

"I know," John smiled. "I've thought of that and I talked to several members of our board of directors about that last night at a dinner. We are not worried. In fact, we are excited. With you and your team managing the integration of the two companies we can realize great strengths from the merger."

Sarah had smiled then. Today, sitting on a mountain top, she grinned wildly. What a great job she had! What a great company Treetop was going to be!

III. TOOLS FOR CHANGE

STRATEGIES TO SUPPORT CHANGE

All the information gathering will be of great interest to no one if the change is not successful. The information collected regarding the change variables is key to the design and implementation of the three change management systems. With the information about the three stages of change and the three key players in the change process, the primary change agents can answer the following questions, resulting in a strong change management plan.

Key Strategies to Support Change

	Leaving the Present	Surviving the Delta State	Reaching the Future
Communication	• Why are we changing? • What happens if we don't change? • Who will change? • What will the changes look like? • What will stay the same? • How does this change fit in with all the other changes? • How will we cope in the delta? • How strong is the sponsorship for this change? • What is expected of everyone? • Are we changing because we've been stupid and made mistakes?	• How will we send the message over and over? • How can we change the words and the tune? • How will we give people a chance to push back? • How will we give people a chance to grieve? • How will we give people constant feedback about where they are in the delta?	• How will we acknowledge the price people have paid during the delta? • How will we show the results of the change? • How will we show what still has to change?

Learning	• What do sponsors have to know/do to support this change?
	• What do change agents have to know/do to support this change?
	• What do targets have to know/do to support this change?
	• What is the target's correct level of competence?
		• How will the trainees balance the training and their current work load?
		• How will the training be modified as the changes change?
			• What further education and training are required?
			  • Refresher
			  • New Hires
			  • Changes to the change

| Rewards/ Reinforcements | • How will the sponsors demonstrate their commitment?
 • How will the sponsorship cascade down/across the organization?
 • How will the current beliefs/behaviors/rules be identified and evaluated?
 • How will the movement from this stage to the next be demonstrated and measured? | • How will targets be involved in the implementation?
 • How will the required resources be identified and made available?
 • What are the milestones in the delta?
 • How will the milestones be celebrated?
 • How will individual behaviors be reinforced?
 • How will resisters who change be rewarded? | • How will the new behaviors/beliefs/rules be institutionalized?
 • How will supporters of the changes become the new heroes?
 • How will success be celebrated? |

Epilogue

This book has been a place to study change and the change process. Completing this book should have given you a solid basis for understanding the elements of change management, garnered from the Element of Change section of each chapter. In addition, you should have the feel of a change project, its complexities, and some of the specific tactics used to manage it from Charlie and Sarah at Treetop in the Real World Example section of each chapter. Their experiences should have helped you to gain insight into how targets, change agents, and sponsors feel about change and what effective change agents do to make change happen successfully. Equally important, you have a set of tools: assessments, planning charts, grids for data collection, in the Tools for Change section at the end of each chapter that will help you with your own changes.

How do you use the knowledge, the insights, the ideas, and the tools you have been reading about? *Comprehensively*. That is, for most companies, a change in the way they manage change. Most change agents know much of what is in this book before they start to read it. But without thinking through the change process in an organized, structured way, they run a great risk of missing something. The changes you and your company are making are too important, too complex, and too vulnerable to give haphazard or casual attention to these issues.

How do you go about a comprehensive, structured, and thorough application of the principles of change management? *Selectively*. The tools presented here are a resource. There are many others as well. Chose those that you find most helpful to you as you assess the three stages of the change process, identify the stakeholders in the project (sponsors, change agents, and targets), and design the three change systems. The tools you use and your selection of them will continue to improve.

There is no magic to change management. There is discipline, commitment, and the intelligent application of knowledge and resources. In some changes that means a conference room the size of a football field papered with Key Role Maps and fishbones and learning system planning charts. In others, it means those same tools sketched on the back of a napkin over lunch.

The size and scope of the change, its relationship to other changes, and the skill and experience of the change agents are key determinants of how change management as a methodology is applied to the change project. Make a decision about where on the continuum of discipline your change project needs to be. Make that decision consciously and with thought. That is a decision with a broad range of options, from football fields to napkins. The decision that is a no-brainier is that the change will be managed by using the knowledge gathered from this book, from your own experiences, and from mentors and models and other reading. The company that does *not* make that decision is in serious jeopardy. It is hoped that it is your competition, not your company, that won't change the way it changes.

Bibliography

Baker, Wayne E. 1994. *Networking Smart.* New York: McGraw-Hill.

Block, Peter. 1993. *Stewardship.* San Francisco: Berrett-Koehler Publishers.

Bridges, William. 1980. *Transitions: Making Sense of Life's Changes.* Reading, MA: Addison-Wesley.

Conner, Daryl R. 1992. *Managing at the Speed of Change.* New York: Villard Books.

Ellis, Christian M., and Elizabeth J. Hawk. 1994. "A Recipe for Success: Redesigning Rewards in Organizations with Mature Teams." *Target* 10, no. 4: 19–27.

Goldman, Steven, Roger Nagel, and Kenneth Proiss. 1994. *Agile Competitors and Virtual Organizations.* New York: Van Nostrand Reinhold.

Greene, Bob. 1994. "Go Metric? Not in this Century." *The Chicago Tribune.* July 25, Section 5, p. 1.

Hammer, Michael, and James Champy. 1993. *Reengineering the Corporation.* New York: Harper Business.

Larkin, T. J., and Sandra Larkin. 1994. *Communicating Change: Winning Employee Support for New Business Goals.* New York: McGraw-Hill.

Lewin, Kurt. 1975. *Field Theory in Social Science.* Westport, CT: Greenwood Press.

Martin, Roger. 1993. "Changing the Mind of the Corporation." *Harvard Business Review.* November–December: 81–94.

McGeary, Johanna, and Cathy Booth. 1993. "Cuba Alone." *Time.* 6 December, 142, no. 24: 42–56.

199

Millstein, Gilbert. 1962. "Why They Walk the High Wire." *The New York Times Magazine*. 4, 16 February, 19–22.

Obradovitch, M. M. and S. E. Stephanou. 1990. *Project Management Risks and Productivity*. Bend, OR: Daniel Spencer.

Peters, Tom. 1987. *Thriving on Chaos: Handbook for Management Revolution*. New York: Alfred A. Knopf.

Peters, Tom. 1992. *Liberation Management: Necessary Disorganization for the Nanosecond Nineties*. New York: Alfred A. Knopf.

Savage, Charles M. 1990. *Fifth Generation Management: Integrating Enterprises through Human Networking*. Bedford, MA: Digital Press.

Senge, Peter M. 1990. *The Fifth Discipline*. New York: Doubleday.

Stegner, Wallace. 1992. *Angle of Repose*. New York: Viking Penguin.

Tomasko, Robert. 1993. *Rethinking the Corporation*. New York: American Management Association.

Appendix:
Professional Associations

Association for Manufacturing Excellence—AME
380 W. Palatine Road
Wheeling, IL 60090
(708) 520-3282

American Production and Inventory Control Society—APICS
500 W. Annandale Road
Falls Church, VA 22046
(800) 444-2742

Society of Manufacturing Engineers—SME
One SME Drive
P.O. Box 930
Dearborn, MI 48121
(313) 271-1500

American Society for Quality Control, Inc.—ASQC
611 E. Wisconsin Avenue
P.O. Box 3005
Milwaukee, WI 53201-3005
(800) 248-1946   U.S.A., Mexico, and Canada
(414) 272-8575

Index